S0-BBO-785

EXPORTS AND LOCAL DEVELOPMENT:
Mexico's New Maquiladoras

EXPORTS AND LOCAL DEVELOPMENT
MEXICO'S NEW MAQUILADORAS

PATRICIA A. WILSON

 University of Texas Press, Austin

The author and publisher are grateful for the permission to use material from the following articles written by the author: "Maquiladoras and Their Transaction Patterns," *Frontera Norte* 5 (1991), a journal of the Colegio de la Frontera Norte in Tijuana, in which a portion of chapter 5 appeared; "The Global Assembly Industry: Maquiladoras in International Perspective," *Journal of Borderlands Studies* 6, no. 2 (1991) 1–32, in which an earlier and shorter version of chapter 2 appeared; "The New Maquiladoras: Flexible Production in Low Wage Regions," in *The Maquiladora Industry: Economic Solution or Problem?*, edited by Khosrow Fatemi (New York: Praeger Publishers, 1990), pp. 135–158, in which a portion of chapter 4 appeared; and "Maquiladoras and Local Linkages: Building Transaction Networks in Guadalajara," reprinted from *Regional and Sectoral Development in Mexico as Alternatives to Migration*, edited by Sergio Diaz-Briquets and Sidney Weintraub, 1991 by permission of Westview Press, Boulder, Colorado, pp. 169–205, in which earlier versions of portions of chapters 5 and 7 appeared.

Requests for permission to reproduce material from this work should be sent to Permissions, University of Texas Press, Box 7819, Austin, TX 78713-7819.

∞ The paper used in this publication meets the minimum requirements of American National Standard for Information Sciences—Permanence of Paper for Printed Library Materials, ANSI Z39.48-1984.

Library of Congress Cataloging-in-Publication Data

Wilson, Patricia Ann.
    Exports and local development : Mexico's new maquiladoras / Patricia Ann Wilson. — 1st ed.
        p. cm.
    Includes bibliographical references (p.   ) and index.
    ISBN 0-292-75144-3.—ISBN 0-292-79074-0 (pbk.)
    1. Offshore assembly industry—Mexico. 2. Flexible manufacturing systems—Mexico. I. Title.
    HD9734.M42W55   1992
    338.4'767'09721—dc20   91-38510
                                                                          CIP

To Vicki, Julia, Dad, and you

Contents

Figures

Map

Tables

Acknowledgments

I would like to thank the many people who helped make this book possible. For funding the field research I wish to thank the Commission on International Migration and Cooperative Economic Development and the University of Texas Research Institute. For assistance in field research I wish to thank Juan José Palacios, Mario Carrillo Huerta, Humberto Lona, Paul Castillo, Alejandro Ibarra, RichAnn Roche, Sandra Wheaton, Deborah Welsheimer Hernandez, Cyrus Reed, and Cesar Zamora. In terms of feedback on the ideas, I wish to thank all those colleagues who commented on drafts of this work, including John Friedmann, Victor Urquidi, Amy Glasmeier, Sidney Weintraub, Sergio Díaz Briquets, Niles Hansen, Bryan Roberts, Juan José Palacios, James Peach, Dilmus James, Eduardo Barrera, and Daniel Nugent. I would also like to thank the students in my graduate seminars on the maquiladora industry, the global assembly industry, and "Taller Jalisco" for their challenging discussions and pertinent fieldwork, both of which helped to shape my thinking on these issues. Thanks are due also to Cheryl Manor for assistance on the manuscript and Gustavo Grad, Cyrus Reed, and Lucy Galbraith for assistance with the graphics. Finally, I would like to thank my colleagues in the School of Architecture and Planning at the University of Texas for the leap of faith in supporting my efforts on this book. By now they can all pronounce *maquiladora* without an accent.

EXPORTS AND LOCAL DEVELOPMENT:
Mexico's New Maquiladoras

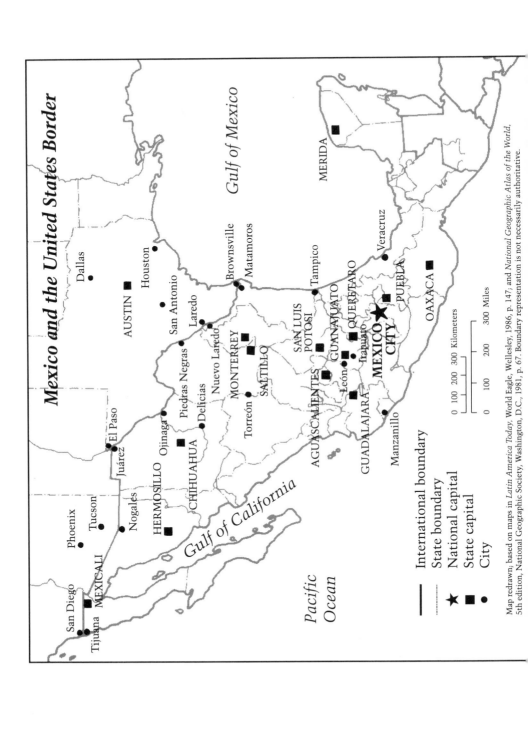

Mexico and the United States Border

Pacific Ocean

Gulf of California

Gulf of Mexico

San Diego
Tijuana
MEXICALI
Phoenix
Tucson
Nogales
El Paso
Juárez
HERMOSILLO
Ojinaga
CHIHUAHUA
Delicias
Piedras Negras
Nuevo Laredo
Laredo
San Antonio
AUSTIN
Houston
Dallas
Brownsville
Matamoros
Torreón
MONTERREY
SALTILLO
Tampico
SAN LUIS
POTOSI
AGUASCALIENTES
GUANAJUATO
QUERETARO
León
Irapuato
GUADALAJARA
Manzanillo
MEXICO
CITY
PUEBLA
Veracruz
OAXACA
MERIDA

International boundary
State boundary
National capital
State capital
City

0   100   200   300 Kilometers
0   100   200   300 Miles

Map redrawn, based on maps in *Latin America Today*, World Eagle, Wellesley, 1986, p. 147, and *National Geographic Atlas of the World*, 5th edition, National Geographic Society, Washington, D.C., 1981, p. 67. Boundary representation is not necessarily authoritative.

1. Introduction and Overview

Visiting an overseas assembly plant in a developing country can fill me with awe. The plant represents the ability of humans to masterplan the production and distribution of goods on a global scale. Corporate planners divide the production process into discrete phases, from research and development, to advanced manufacturing, to routine manufacturing, searching the globe for optimal locations, weaving them into a complicated web of worldwide logistics and communications. Advanced and developing countries are intertwined in a global production network. Conditions and events in one place affect those in another in a dramatically visible way. Instantaneous communication and worldwide supply lines bring global unity into sharp focus.

Viewing the work process inside the assembly plant gives me different impressions, depending on the many forms that assembly plants take. Here are three very different views I have witnessed:

In a hot, stifling, poorly lighted Quonset hut on the Mexican border where shoes are assembled for well-known U.S. department stores, the noxious fumes overwhelmed me as I watched the women and men work. Using sewing machines, thread, and leather from the United States, rows of women stitched tops to soles. Some men attached heels to shoes with hot glue in rapid succession, while others deftly removed excess rubber from the heel by turning the shoe around the sharp blade of a trimmer with their hands, rapidly, mechanically, under the gaze of the Virgin's image pasted on the machine to remind them that they are human.

In another Mexican city I visited a well-lighted air-conditioned electronics factory with row after row of women inserting scores of tiny colored pieces into circuit boards in just the right order. At break time they doffed the colored robes that indicate their seniority to reveal attractive dresses and high heels. "We come to get out of the house, to socialize, to meet men, not just to support our families," one young line worker told me. On the other side of the factory floor was a new automated high density double-sided insertion machine, attended by one man.

In an auto parts assembly plant I saw young men working in teams aided by machines to stamp, bend, weld, and paint materials. Each team was responsible for an entire subassembly. Not far away in a clearing on the shop floor a soundproof room housed a blackboard where line workers are encouraged to meet with their team managers to discuss production problems and suggest alternative solutions. A hand-written diagnosis was still on the board from the last occupants.

These sights—common in Mexico, the Caribbean, and Asia—raise a debate about whether the global assembly industry is good or bad, usually pitting labor, environmental, and women's groups on the one side against business groups on the other. The former accuse the global assembly industry of being exploitative; putting the worst part of the industrial process in poor countries; taking advantage of their low wage rates, the young inexperienced female labor force, and loose environmental regulations; and stealing jobs from workers in the advanced countries. The business groups argue that the global assembly industry allows multinational firms to remain competitive in the world market, thereby benefitting the home country, and that it is natural for assembly industry to go offshore as wage rates rise in the advanced countries and industries mature. The debate gets louder and louder but never closer to being resolved.

I believe that neither side is totally correct: The spread of the assembly industry is not "natural." It is the result of human decisions, in both the public and private sectors. These decisions can be influenced and changed. How the global assembly industry behaves in a particular country—and even whether or not it exists there—depends to a great extent on local public policy, local private sector initiatives, and local labor practices. Neither is it certain that a strategy of minimizing labor costs enhances the long-term competitiveness of industry when compared to other strategies that increase productivity and flexibility. On the other side of the argument, neither are global assembly plants more exploitative than most other capitalist enterprises. They normally pay prevailing wage rates and abide by local environmental regulations.

Not only are both sides partly wrong, the debate is not helpful. It is couched in the terms of a zero sum game: Third World workers win at the expense of First World workers, capital wins at the expense of labor, one country wins at the expense of another, we win at your expense or vice-versa.

I wish to focus the debate differently, on how host countries can shape and utilize the global assembly industry to further their own internal development. Such a debate recognizes that a global capitalist economy is in sway for the foreseeable future and that the task is not to criticize it but to find practical ways in which to use it for positive ends. Can the global assembly industry stimulate more than just dead-end low wage jobs and foreign exchange? Can it create linkages with the host country's economy that help diversify its industrial structure and produce an array of productive jobs with upward mobility for its own labor force? If it can, the advanced countries would benefit as well, since larger internal markets in the poor countries would reduce migration to the rich countries, easing competition for jobs in the rich countries and making the host countries more desirable trading partners.

The age of ideology is over. Confrontation and conflict are too costly for the world to sustain. Globalization is bringing down political borders, ideological borders, economic borders, and cultural borders. More and more countries try to compete in the global market, opening up their borders to the ebbs and flows of international capital, often at great social cost of lowering incomes and increasing inequality. Is this high social cost a necessary part of globalization? Will globalization be at the service of humankind, or vice-versa? Will we be able to turn globalization into a positive trend, one that expands opportunity for all people and brings us together without denying our individual uniqueness? Or will it be a negative trend that takes advantage of differences for the good of a few at the expense of the majority?

The rise of the global assembly industry is part of the globalization process. More and more developing countries are jumping on the bandwagon of global assembly, or trying to, as they search for new roles in the international economy. Can assembly industry be more than just a source of low skilled low wage jobs? Can it create linkages with the urban, regional, and national economy where it is located and be the catalyst for more diversified economic development?

This book is devoted to advancing this new debate—how to turn export-oriented assembly industry in developing countries into a catalyst for more integrated local development. This refocussed debate holds great relevance for the current discussions on the proposed free trade agreement between Mexico and the United States. In many ways the assembly industry in Mexico is a precursor of the free trade agreement, offering a preview of the division of labor that free trade between advanced and developing countries would generate.

To find a role for the assembly industry in local development requires an understanding of the changing nature of the assembly industry. A main thesis of this book is that the assembly industry, as experienced in Mexico, has changed dramatically since the early 1980s in many ways. No longer is it simply the low skilled, labor intensive, largely feminine assembly activity that it once was. Second generation maquiladoras now incorporate much more advanced technology, more capital intensive methods, a more masculine labor force, and more manufacturing. How do these changes affect the ability of the assembly industry to become a catalyst for integrated internal development, as happened in the Asian "tigers"?

The other main thesis of the book is that public policy in the host country can have some impact on how well the assembly industry integrates with the local economy. There is room for public policy in Mexico to substantially increase local linkages from the assembly industry. Policy initiatives must take into account the changing nature of assembly industry, which has been influenced by the rise of a new corporate strategy called flexible manufacturing. The new assembly plants, called *maquiladoras*, incorporate many of the production and management methods of flexible manufacturing. Yet flexible production generates even fewer linkages on the whole than more labor intensive production. The new maquiladoras with greater potential for creating local linkages are local Mexican-owned firms, located mainly in the interior, that are restructuring to enter the export market. By analyzing sourcing patterns and building local transactional networks, the Mexican government can increase the local linkages not only of the locally owned maquiladoras but also of some of the foreign-owned maquiladoras. In Guadalajara the sector of locally owned craft producers and the sector of foreign-owned electronics producers show particular potential.

Chapter 2 traces the rise of the global assembly industry, looking at changing corporate strategy and host country conditions. It addresses two major questions: Why has so much of the developing world (e.g., most of Latin America) heretofore been passed over by the international assembly industry? Why have only a few countries (specifically, the four Asian "tigers") been able to use assembly industry as a springboard to broader export-led industrialization by creating local linkages? The chapter then draws out the national policy implications for Mexico to be able to create more local linkages from its maquiladora industry.

Chapter 3 traces the development of the Mexican assembly industry, from its beginnings as a regional development program in the 1960s to the dramatic take-off point in 1982 when it became an important part of the new national strategy for export-led industrialization. It describes the recent Mexican government initiatives to promote the maquiladora industry. Using the latest Mexican government data, the chapter discusses post-1982 changes in location patterns, sectoral composition, and labor force. The data show that the maquiladoras in the interior create more local linkages than do those of the border, because they use more domestic inputs.

Chapter 4 first sets the historical and conceptual framework for understanding the new corporate strategy of flexible manufacturing and its implications for low wage assembly in Mexico. It discusses the increasing use of Japanese-led innovations in flexibility, such as programmable machinery, quality circles, and just-in-time inventory methods. It analyzes the hypothesis that flexible manufacturing will bring industry back home from its Third World outposts. Drawing on my survey of over seventy maquiladora plants along the border and in the interior, the chapter sheds new empirical light on the extent to which maquiladoras are adopting flexible production methods in technology, management techniques, shop floor organization, and interfirm relationships. It documents whether the use of flexible production methods brings higher or lower use of Mexican-made inputs.

Drawing on the survey results, chapter 5 analyzes the kinds of local and domestic linkages the maquiladoras generate. Using an analysis of the plants' transaction patterns, three kinds of linkages are examined: purchasing goods and services from local and national suppliers, selling output on the local and domestic market, and creating local spin-off firms. To explain the relatively high degree of domestic inputs among interior assembly plants, this chapter provides an in-depth case study of the assembly industry in Guadalajara, based on survey results from all twenty-six maquiladoras located there. The transactional networks identified for the maquiladoras in Guadalajara are then contrasted with those identified for Monterrey and the border region.

Chapter 6 provides case studies of twenty-seven individual plants selected from the interior and the border. The case studies bring out the anecdotal richness of the motivations, problems, and efforts of plant managers in operating where they do, adopting new technologies and management methods, and using local suppliers. Cases include large U.S. and Japanese maquiladoras in electronics and auto parts, small locally owned crafts producers, and joint ventures in glass and metal products.

Chapter 7 points out the need for the Mexican public sector to develop finely tuned local efforts, in addition to supportive national policy, to stimulate local linkages. The analysis of the maquiladoras' transaction patterns indicates that potential supplier relationships are going unrealized among firms in the same sector and same city. While the initiative for linking these firms should come from the firms themselves, the public sector can play a catalyzing role. The chapter describes how effective local networks have been forged among crafts producers and electronics firms in other countries and applies the findings to the case of Guadalajara.

Whether increasing global unity, as exemplified by the international assembly industry, is a positive force for humanity depends on the efforts we make to use it wisely. There is no predetermined outcome.

2. The Global Assembly Industry: Maquiladoras in International Perspective

Throughout its twenty-five year history the maquiladora industry has remained largely an enclave industry, using inputs from the United States and integrating very little with the Mexican economy. Yet in other parts of the globe, the foreign assembly industry has been a catalyst, a stepping stone, to further industrialization and higher wage rates in the host country. The newly industrializing countries of Asia—Korea, Taiwan, Hong Kong, and Singapore—are prime examples. If the maquiladora industry begins to follow suit—as the Mexican government is encouraging—it should gradually integrate itself more deeply into the Mexican economy.

Nevertheless, there is no natural, inexorable path to advanced industrialization based on the assembly industry. The reason why some countries have been able to develop on the basis of assembly industry and some have not has to do with public policy, the social and political context, and the historical period. The following discussion of the rise of the global assembly industry addresses the conditions and factors that helped to create the success of some of the Asian countries, relegate the Caribbean to traditional assembly, and put Mexico in a role somewhere between the two extremes. While some of the propitious conditions and factors could be replicated consciously in Mexico to take greater advantage of the assembly industry, there is no assurance that the assembly industry will automatically evolve into a more integrated industrial base.

The Rise of the Global Assembly Industry

Offshore assembly in developing countries started in the 1950s in Hong Kong and Puerto Rico,[1] followed in the 1960s by Taiwan, Singapore, Philippines, Mexico, and the Dominican Republic (see Table 1). Following the example of Shannon airport in Ireland,[2] many

Table 1 The Spread of Export Processing in the Third World, 1960–1984 (by country and date of establishment of first export-processing facilities)

	1960–1964	1965–1969	1970–1974	1975–1979	1980–1984
Asia	Hong Kong	South Korea Taiwan Singapore Philippines India	Malaysia	Indonesia Sri Lanka	China Thailand Bangladesh Pakistan
Latin America and Caribbean	Puerto Rico	Mexico Dominican Republic Panama Brazil	Haiti El Salvador Guatemala Colombia	Jamaica Honduras Nicaragua Chile	Costa Rica
Africa and Middle East		Mauritius	Tunisia Jordan	Egypt Syria Liberia Senegal	Cyprus

Source: Currie (1984: 5), supplemented by country-specific information.

of these governments set up special industrial parks, called export-processing zones, in order to attract foreign investment. Within the boundaries of these zones, firms were allowed to process goods for export without paying duties on imported components. Hong Kong, following its tradition as a commercial entrepôt, or free trade zone, designated the entire island as an export-processing zone. By the end of the sixties, eleven developing countries had an export-processing zone. By the end of the seventies there were fifty-seven zones in twenty-nine countries. By the mid-eighties there were seventy-nine zones in thirty-five countries, with substantial assembly activity occurring outside designated zones as well (Currie 1984). Asia accounts for over half (55 percent) of the world's zone employment; Mexico, the Caribbean, and Central America about 30 percent (with Mexico representing over half that amount); South America (Brazil, Colombia, and Chile) about 8 percent; and Africa, the Mediterranean, and the Middle East account for the small remainder (see Table 2). The main products are electronics (both consumer goods and components), textiles, apparel, and footwear (see Table 3).

Corporate Strategy

The rise of international assembly in the late sixties was not an isolated curiosity; rather, it was a bellwether event evidencing a deep-seated change in the global political economy which many authors refer to as the "new international division of labor" (e.g., Frobel, Heinrichs, and Kreye 1980; Bluestone and Harrison 1982; Moulaert and Salinas 1983). The rise of global assembly reflected the decline of U.S. corporate hegemony in the world economy, the rise of foreign competition, and the search for new competitive strategies.

In the face of the rising foreign competition, U.S. multinational corporations had two broad strategy choices: to improve productivity or reduce costs.[3] On a national level, workers' wage increases were beginning to outpace diminishing productivity gains. Many corporations chose a cost reduction strategy focusing on labor costs. Third World countries that offered low-cost, plentiful (and female)[4] labor became very attractive locations—not as an access point to the local market, but as a site for carrying out labor-intensive processing of goods destined for the international market. Thus as textile, garment, shoe, and toy production went offshore along with the assembly of electronic components and electronic consumer goods, the new international division of labor was born.[5] It seemed

Table 2 *Principal Host Countries, 1978–1983 (by continent and amount of employment in export processing)*

Place	Export-processing Employment 1978 No.	%	1983 No.	%
Asia	360,700	56%	478,500	55%
Singapore	105,000		105,000	
Taiwan	77,400		83,400	
Hong Kong	59,600		70,000	
Malaysia	56,000		101,000	
South Korea	33,000		33,000	
Philippines	19,700		24,700	
Latin America and Caribbean	246,100	38%	335,200	39%
Mexico[a]	90,700	14%	150,900	17%
Caribbean and Central America[b]	108,800	17%	120,000	14%
Haiti	87,900		87,900	
Dominican Republic[c]	11,500		21,400	
South America	47,200	6%	64,300	7%
Brazil	43,800		60,000	
Africa and Middle East	39,200	6%	52,700	6%
Mauritius	17,400		28,900	
Tunis	10,000	——	10,000	——
Total	646,000	100%	866,000	100%

Source: Currie (1984), except as noted.
[a]Mexican data from Secretaría de Programación y Presupuesto (SPP).
[b]Does not include several small East Caribbean islands.
[c]Dominican Republic data from the National Council of Industrial Free Zones, reported in Thoumi (1988).

to reflect the pinnacle of mass production rationality carried to an international scale (see chapter 4).[6]

Among developed countries, U.S. multinationals were the primary ones to pursue the global assembly strategy. A lack of protectionist sentiment at home made offshore sourcing politically feasible. Existing U.S. tariff codes (Items 806 and 807) provided a tax incentive by allowing the U.S. components in the assembled products to be reimported duty free (see chapter 3).

Table 3 *Sectoral Composition of Export-processing Industry (by percentage of firms in each sector)*

	Clothing and Textiles		Electronics		Other	
	1978 %	1983 %	1978 %	1983 %	1978 %	1983 %
Asia (except Hong Kong)	16	15	45	33	39	53
Hong Kong	32	31	4	5	64	64
Caribbean and Central America	61	38	13	21	27	42
Mexico	33	27	47	39	20	33
South America	50	35	0	0	50	65
Africa and Middle East	41	41	2	1	57	58
Average[a]	26	21	38	31	36	49

Source: Based on data from Currie (1984: 24, Table 4) which are aggregated from individual zone level data for twenty-three countries.
[a] Based on all reporting firms.

European multinationals did not face the same pressures as U.S. corporations to reduce costs because of tariff barriers helping to protect the European Community from foreign competition (Grunwald and Flamm 1985). Moreover, European producers had access to large pools of inexpensive migrant labor without going offshore. There were also lower labor cost countries within Europe—Ireland, Portugal, Spain—that served as assembly sites for some industries. Nevertheless, the Europeans did have a presence in the global assembly industry, primarily in North Africa and the Mediterranean.

Japanese corporations carved out their comparative advantage largely on the basis of productivity increases stemming from the introduction of flexible manufacturing—not just new technology, but new management methods and shop floor organization, along with an emphasis on quality (see chapter 4). Thus they did not grow to depend on low cost labor locations as much as U.S. industry did. Yet, like the Europeans, the Japanese did have a presence in the global assembly industry, especially in Taiwan, South Korea, and Malaysia. In fact, by the end of the 1970s their investment in electronics manufacturing in East Asia was growing rapidly, even though most of it was aimed at regional or third-party markets and consisted of older technologies (Grunwald and Flamm 1985).

Sectoral Patterns

Improvements in international communication and transportation made a global production strategy feasible for certain products and industries: those with high value-to-weight ratios such as textiles (including garments) and electronic components. Electronic component assembly was the first U.S. industry to go offshore en masse in response to Japanese competition. The feasibility of offshore locations for electronics came about with the development of integrated circuits etched on silicon chips in the late sixties.[7] While the manufacture of the chips was capital intensive, their assembly and encapsulation were not. Given the high value-to-weight ratios and improvements in air transport and telecommunications, the labor intensive portion could be geographically separated.[8] U.S. producers of electronic consumer goods—radios, tape recorders, televisions—also began to locate their labor intensive assembly operations abroad in the face of Japanese competition. Television components and subassemblies became the second largest 806/807 import to the United States from developing countries after semiconductors (Grunwald and Flamm 1985: 18). By the early 1980s the remaining U.S. television manufacturers sourced virtually all of their subassemblies from their overseas operations—mainly Mexico, but also Taiwan and later Singapore.[9]

U.S. producers of textiles, apparel, and shoes faced increasing competition in the sixties from inexpensive but high quality imports (especially from Hong Kong and elsewhere in Southeast Asia). With a declining supply of low-wage female workers in the United States, many textile, apparel, and shoe manufacturers opted to take their most labor intensive operations abroad to cheaper labor locations in order to compete with these imports. The stable and relatively unsophisticated production technology (even though the product designs were volatile and sophisticated), the high value-to-weight ratios of the products, and the separability of the labor intensive stitching from the design and cutting stages made this strategy feasible. Mexico and the Caribbean became the principal recipients of U.S. textile, apparel, and shoe assembly operations. They used almost exclusively U.S.-made materials to maintain high quality standards and qualify for 806/807 tax exemptions on the imported final products.[10]

The rise of the international assembly industry was the result of many individual corporate strategic decisions about how to deal with intensifying international competition. Yet they fit together into a pattern—by no means a natural or inexorable one—of opting for cost competition based on reducing direct labor costs. Many corporations found a strategy to deal with growing foreign competition not by substituting capital for labor, not by reorganizing the shop floor to increase worker productivity, not by bringing in low cost labor through migrant flows from the Third World (although this indeed has been increasing; see Sassen 1988), but rather by going offshore to Third World locations. Compared to the primary Japanese strategy of increasing long-term productivity by adopting flexible manufacturing methods, the predominant U.S. strategy of labor cost cutting was a short-term one. This pattern reflected, and in fact exacerbated, declining U.S. economic hegemony (see chapter 4).

Geographic Patterns

If the global assembly industry is following a natural pattern of spreading to ever cheaper labor countries, as the product cycle theorists presume, why is it that so many developing countries have been passed over? The bulk of foreign assembly activity (about 87 percent) is concentrated in East and Southeast Asia, Mexico, and the Caribbean. Table 2 shows that the regional percentages have scarcely changed over time (although individual country shares within regions have).

Of particular interest for the Mexican comparison is why the rest of Latin America has been relatively untouched by assembly industry. There are many Latin American countries that offer plentiful, low wage, and dexterous female (and male) workers. And the distance argument (i.e., that South American countries are too distant from the United States compared to Mexico and the Caribbean) pales in the light of Asia's attractiveness.

There is one overriding reason why most of Latin America was overlooked by multinational corporations seeking assembly sites for reexport in the 1960s. It was the deep, prolonged commitment to import substitution as the primary industrial development strategy adopted by most Latin American governments. More precisely, it was the social relations (or what some would call the "business climate") forged by and forging the import substitution approach.

Ironically, the strategy of import substitution in Latin America was mostly complementary to, and supportive of, U.S. multinational interests during the post–World War II boom when lack of markets had been the fundamental impediment to their growth. The protectionist barriers of import substitution nurtured domestic markets, however fledgling. The import substitution strategy spawned an urban industrial labor force and a mushrooming middle class. The middle class included the expanding ranks of white-collar government employees needed to plan the industrial infrastructure, educate the workers, and manage the public enterprises underpinning urban industrial expansion.[11] Instead of exporting final products to these countries, the multinational enterprises invested directly in factories and final assembly plants to supply the domestic markets from within the trade barriers. They also sold intermediate inputs and technology to the growing market of locally owned industries.

What then explained the sudden aversion to import substitution by corporations looking for assembly sites for reexport? Some corporations began to perceive foreign competition in the increasingly global market as a more threatening bottleneck to growth than the lack of markets. These companies began to look for an inexpensive and disciplined labor force in order to reduce labor costs. But in Latin America the import substitution strategy had created populist demands to share the fruits of industrialization with the rapidly unionizing industrial workers, the growing urban middle class, and the flux of rural migrants expanding the ranks of the urban poor. A frequent result in Latin American countries was a populist government willing to (or forced to) share the gains with these mobilized social sectors—through public spending, overvalued currencies, or direct wage and salary increases. Thus the Latin American countries that had wholeheartedly pursued import substitution—with the encouragement of U.S. foreign aid through the Alliance for Progress—were not attractive to multinationals as labor intensive assembly sites for reexport. These corporations needed a labor force that did not expect—or was in no position to demand—an increasing share of the pie.

Hong Kong, Taiwan, Singapore, and South Korea fulfilled that need well for multinational corporations for whom the distance was not an insurmountable problem. While three of these four countries did pursue import substitution, the fundamental difference is that the governments were able to prevent import substitution from becoming a vehicle for populist demands. They maintained an authoritarian control over the labor force and middle classes throughout their import substitution experience that carried over rather easily to their export manufacturing efforts. Moreover, all but the government of Hong Kong maintained a strong active involvement in the economy—a striking contrast to the Chicago School or Thatcher neoliberal approach characterized by laissez-faire and so often associated with export-led strategies. Even Hong Kong, with its nationalized land and subsidized housing stock, was far from laissez-faire.

Singapore. The island economy of Singapore had only a brief flirtation with import substitution, from independence in 1959 to 1965, following its British colonial role as a free port for trade between the Indian Ocean and the Pacific. During this interlude with import substitution, the government of Singapore swiftly routed Communist influence in the labor movement and established a single officially recognized (and controlled) union. The government rejected the import substitution strategy in 1965, when expulsion from the Malaysian Federation and the British decision to close its military bases left it without hopes for a sizeable internal market. The city-state then adopted a full-fledged national strategy of export-oriented industrialization based on foreign assembly industry. It improved the roads, public utilities, telecommunications networks, and airports; it built an industrial estate with nearby public housing; it enacted tax incentives and investment guarantees for foreign investors (Griffith 1987). But the central girder to its efforts was to control the labor force: "The government believed that the success of the (export) industrialization programmes rested on low wages and a disciplined work-force" (Chen 1983: 12). In 1968 the government passed laws to increase the work week, reduce vacation and sick leave, reduce eligibility for overtime pay, and remove a broad range of labor issues from collective bargaining. In that same year Singapore attracted its first electronics corporation, the semiconductor industry leader Fairchild (see Table 4).[12]

Taiwan. By the end of fifty years of Japanese colonial rule in 1945, Taiwan had developed a light industrial base along with some heavy industries such as aluminum, chemicals, and shipbuilding, largely through investments by leading Japanese family groups (Ho, cited in Cumings 1984: 13). The colonial bureaucracy had developed into a strong state, with tight police and military control which helped to isolate it from middle- and working-class demands. In the absence of a local entrepreneurial class, the state played a large role in directing the economy. The Japanese family investment groups and the strong state repressed the Taiwanese labor force, "leading in the 1940s to a forced military-style discipline in the factories" (Cumings 1984: 15).

The postwar emergence of single party rule by the Kuomintang (KMT)[13] kept the centralized and powerful bureaucracy the Japanese had left behind largely intact. The KMT added its own sizable military force to ensure state autonomy and avoid democratic par-

Table 4 *U.S. Corporations with Semiconductor Assembly Plants in the Third World (by country and year of establishment)*

Country	Year	Corporation
Hong Kong	1961	Fairchild
		Carter
Taiwan	1964	General Instrument
		Philco-Ford
		RTW
	1967	RCA
	1969	Philips
	1970	Texas Instruments
Korea	1964	Fairchild
	1965	Motorola
		Signatics
	1970	American Micro
	1971	Varadyne
Singapore	1968	Fairchild
	1969	Air Reduction
		SGS
		Stemen
		Continental Services
	1970	Texas Instruments
		National
		Intersel
	1971	Electronic Array
Mexico	1968	Fairchild
		Transitron
	1969	Motorola
		American Micro
		General Instrument
	1970	Sprague

Source: Chang (1971: 43), based on field interviews.

ticipation (and to entertain the hopes of someday retaking the mainland). The government continued to repress labor harshly, outlawing unions and imposing martial law, which lasted from 1947 to 1986.

The United States supported the KMT with generous foreign aid, both economic and military. To bolster Japanese economic (but not military) influence in the region as a buffer to Communist influence, the United States wanted to groom Taiwan as a permanent economic periphery, providing labor, markets, and raw materials for Japan (Cumings 1984: 15–22). U.S. aid missions assisted Taiwan's national planning efforts for agricultural and industrial development.

The KMT—with at least tacit approval if not always active support by the U.S. aid missions—adopted an import substitution strategy. The government used protective tariffs and overvalued exchange rates to nurture selected industries such as textiles, cement, and glass. Forging a strong link between the state and the private sector, the KMT granted monopolies to favored entrepreneurs, usually mainlanders, who took over industries formerly held by Japanese family groups. After the peak of easy import substitution in 1958–59, the government opted for an export-led strategy to utilize Taiwan's comparative advantage of inexpensive, yet educated, labor. While this strategic change from import substitution to export orientation has occurred at great social expense and political upheaval in Latin America, it happened quickly and easily in Taiwan.

To implement the export-led strategy, the Taiwan government in 1960 devalued the currency to cheapen exports (and the labor used to make the exports), reduced tariff barriers, created tax incentives for exporters, and provided state guarantees to protect foreign investments. In 1965 Taiwan opened an export-processing zone at Kaohsiung to further attract multinational assembly plants. These steps were taken in the context of long-range planning by the state.

Korea.   Korea experienced a similar history to Taiwan's, but with more social disruption. Japanese colonial rule from 1910 to 1945 created in Korea—as in Taiwan—an independent, militarized, repressive authoritarian state that in the 1930s adopted national planning to industrialize the colony. The state protected and subsidized chosen industries (and the Japanese family investment groups that operated them), with heavy industry in the north, such as steel, chemicals, and hydroelectric power, and light industry in the south, where the best rice-producing lands were to be found. Under Soviet auspices, North Korea reacted to the lifting of Japanese control in 1945 with a social revolution, during which many northern entrepreneurs, professionals, and educated workers fled to the south. Under U.S. influence, the southern landlords held the state in the south, maintaining power by police and military force without promoting economic development. The civil war from 1950 to 1953 left South Korea clearly under U.S. hegemony and slated to play the same role as Taiwan: an economic periphery to foster Japanese economic growth.

The United States channeled massive amounts of economic and military assistance to the new South Korean government under Syngman Rhee. South Korea pursued import substitution just a few years behind Taiwan, protecting key industries with overvalued exchange rates and protective tariffs and eliminating the influence of the landlords through land reform. As in Taiwan, the authoritarian government, heavily militarized with U.S. support, enforced a regimented discipline in the factories, keeping women workers at the bottom of the economic ladder. The state chose favored Korean families to take over Japanese industries and build up their wealth through state-protected monopolies. The huge military was used to stifle democratic demands but at the same time provided upward mobility and training to future bureaucrats and corporate managers (Cumings 1984: 22–26).

The phase of easy import substitution ended in South Korea in the early 1960s when protectionist barriers and domestic demand were no longer sufficient to spawn new industries. Unlike in Taiwan, however, the transition to an export-led phase was violent. The military cleared the way with a coup in 1961.[14] By 1964 the military government under Park Chung Hee had devalued the Korean currency, removed tariff barriers, promoted tax incentives for exports, and provided guarantees and transportation cost subsidies to foreign investors. To further attract foreign corporations, the government opened an export-processing zone in Masan in 1965. As in Taiwan, these steps were taken in the context of long-range planning by the state, through the Economic Planning Board (similar to the famous Japanese ministry of industry and trade, MITI). Park created the Korean CIA to ensure the party's power and autonomy. The KCIA, as an arm of the executive, eventually "penetrated nearly every arena of Korean life, with agents in factories, central and local government offices, and university classrooms" (Cumings 1984: 29).

Thus in both Korea and Taiwan the rise of export processing came on the heels of import substitution. Yet unlike the Latin American experience, the import substitution phase in Korea and Taiwan never included the workers or middle classes in a competition for political power. Repressive, authoritarian governments excluded them in the 1950s under import substitution and easily continued to exclude them in the 1960s under the export-led strategy. Moreover, the Taiwanese and Korean governments maintained a tight control over, and involvement in, the economy during both import substitution and the export-orientation phases.

Hong Kong.   This British crown colony has never pursued an import substitution strategy. By the 1950s, with an open economy from over a century of experience as a free port for international commerce, Hong Kong could easily take advantage of its international transportation, communication, and banking infrastructure to promote the export of light manufactures. In the late 1940s and early 1950s China's social upheavals produced an influx into Hong Kong of capital, entrepreneurs, and skilled workers—especially in the textile industry—which further set the stage for manufactured exports. With the absence of minimum wage regulations and scant union activity, foreign capital was already finding Hong Kong a haven for export processing by the late 1950s (Fajnzylber 1981: 121, 126; Lin and Ho 1980: 11, cited in Fajnzylber 1981).[15] While not as overtly repressive as in Taiwan and South Korea, labor legislation in Hong Kong banned general unions, sympathy strikes, and political strikes (Henderson 1989: 136). The government played an important role in the economy, but one that was largely supportive of the needs of private capital; for example, by subsidizing the private cost of labor through free public training, welfare payments, and subsidized housing (Taylor and Kwok 1989).

Latin America and the Caribbean. In light of Latin America's experience with import substitution, the question becomes not why was so much of Latin America passed over by the international assembly industry, but, rather, why did international assembly industry come to Latin America at all? One could also ask, in light of the social and political relations of import substitution in Latin America, why did any of these countries even try to attract an industry built on low cost, disciplined labor with few domestic linkages?

First, with the exception of Puerto Rico and Haiti, none of the initial efforts to attract assembly industry in Latin America was part of a full-fledged effort to promote a national strategy of export manufacturing.[16] Second, the efforts that were made involved relatively few countries in Latin America and usually originated as a development strategy for a particular region—an undeveloped region (e.g., Manaus in the Brazilian Amazon),[17] a labor surplus region (e.g., Mexico's northern border region after the United States halted the bracero program for Mexican farmworkers), or a geopolitically strategic region (e.g., Arica and Punta Arenas in the northern and southern border zones of Chile). In each case the export-processing efforts were tangential to an overall import substitution strategy. Even the tiny Caribbean nations (except Haiti) that pursued assembly firms continued to depend on either raw material exports or import substitution for the mainstay of their economy (see Table 5).

Table 5 *Export-processing Zones in Latin America and the Caribbean*

	Date Established	No of Mfg. Firms	Main Industries
LATIN AMERICA			
Brazil			
Manaus	1968	200 in 1983	electric and electronic appliances
Chile			
Iquique	1978	0 in 1983	
Punta Arenas	1975	2 in 1983	textiles, cannery
Colombia			
Palmaseca	1970	13 in 1984	shoes, apparel
Barranquilla	1971	32 in 1983	textiles, metal work
Cúcuta	1972	2 in 1983	shoes, wood products
Buenaventura	1973	n.a.	
Santa Marta	1974	5 in 1984	apparel, shoes
Cartagena	1982	4 in 1984	wood products
Costa Rica[a]			
Moin	n.a.	3 in 1982	apparel, electronics
El Salvador			
San Bartolo	1974	9 in 1983	apparel, electronics
Guatemala[b]			
Santo Tomás de Castillo	1972	3 in 1984	sporting goods, textiles
Honduras[c]			
Puerto Cortés	1978	5 in 1982	apparel, furniture
Mexico[d]			
Border Region	1966	622 in 1984	electronics, shoes, apparel
Nicaragua			
Las Mercedes	1976	3 in 1978 0 in 1984	clothing
Puerto Rico			
Mayagüez	1962	9 in 1983	textiles, meat processing

Table 5 *Continued*

	Date Established	No of Mfg. Firms	Main Industries
Panama			
Colón	1969	3 in 1984	bicycle assembly
CARIBBEAN			
Barbados (9 EPZs)	n.a.	19 in 1988	apparel, electronics
Dominican Republic (16 EPZs)	n.a.	235 in 1988	apparel, shoes, electronics
Haiti (2 EPZs)	n.a.	40 in 1988	apparel, sporting goods, electronics
Jamaica (4 EPZs)	n.a.	36 in 1988	apparel, food processing
OECS[e] (9 EPZs)	n.a.	67 in 1988	apparel, electronics

Source: Currie (1984); U.S. Department of Commerce, Caribbean Basin Initiative Office (1989).
[a]By 1988 Costa Rica had nine free zones with forty firms, 40 percent of which were U.S.-owned, and 5,035 employees.
[b]By 1988, the Guatemalan zone had ten firms, three of which were U.S.-owned.
[c]By 1988, the Honduran zone had twenty-six firms, 30 percent U.S.-owned, with 3,874 employees.
[d]The border region in Mexico refers to the thirty-one-kilometer strip along the U.S. border.
[e]Organization of eastern Caribbean states—data cover Antigua, Dominica, Grenada, St. Kitts, St. Lucia, and St. Vincent.

What prompted foreign investors to set up assembly industries in Latin America? The bulk of early assembly investment in Latin America went to Mexico and Haiti (Table 2). Wages in Mexico (counting mandatory benefits) were double those in Asia in 1970 (Table 6). Nevertheless, the proximity of Mexico brought firms from the United States that could not go to Asia—small firms and firms whose products had low value-to-weight ratios. Also, Mexico attracted large multinationals that wanted to spread their country risk by locating additional assembly plants outside of Asia; for example, Fairchild Semiconductor, Motorola, and General Instrument (see Table 4).[18]

Table 6 *Wage Differences in Electronics Assembly by Country, 1970 (average hourly earnings, including supplementary compensation in U.S. dollars)*

Country	Semiconductors	Consumer Electronics
Taiwan	n.a.	$ .14
Hong Kong	$ .28	.27
Singapore	.29	n.a.
Jamaica	.30	n.a.
Korea	.33	n.a.
Mexico	.61	.53
Ireland	.70	n.a.
Dutch Antilles	.72	n.a.
Japan	1.30	.58
Canada	2.11	3.50
United States	2.97	2.69

Source: Compiled from U.S. Tariff Commission, *Economic Factors Affecting the Use of Items 807.00 and 806.30 of the Tariff Schedule of the U.S.*, Washington, D.C., 1970, p. A-90, reported in Chang (1971: 27).

Haiti was a clear departure from the Latin American norm of import substitution and labor mobilization. "Papa Doc" Duvalier, the corrupt and repressive dictator from 1957 until his death in 1971, began an all-out recruitment of foreign assembly industry in the late 1960s. Boasting the lowest wages in the Western Hemisphere,[19] the Duvalier regime repressed all union activity in order to maintain the country's comparative advantage in attracting foreign investment. Duvalier's son, continuing in his father's steps, established an industrial park for foreign assembly plants in the capital city of Port-au-Prince near the country's leading airport and seaport. Assembly industry became the engine of Haiti's remarkable economic growth during the 1970s. From the stagnation of the 1950s and 1960s, Haiti reached a rate of growth of GNP of nearly 6 percent in 1973, while annual construction growth topped 13 percent (Garrity 1974: 208). Assembly industry continued to grow in Haiti until the early 1980s, when social and political unrest could no longer be contained. "Baby Doc" was overthrown in 1986.[20]

Thus, with few exceptions, the difference in social relations attendant upon import-substituting industrialization in Latin America and Asia was the main reason why Latin America has played such a small role in the international assembly industry and Asia such a large one. As Ruth Pearson (1986: 74) aptly states, "Latin American industrialisation strategy represented a different political project from that pursued in SE Asia: a political project which has seen organised labour play a major role. Although this often resulted in the defeat of the labour movement—frequently via the intervention and repression of the military—it never wiped out the tradition of the organised industrial working class in Mexico, Chile, Argentina, Brazil and Colombia, which was based on the expansion of domestic industry." Far from a natural spread of mature industries and their labor intensive processes to ever cheaper labor locations around the globe, the rise of the global assembly industry is a story of corporate strategy and specific social, economic, and political relationships.

Linkages

The Extent of Local Linkages in the Asian Tigers

From the host country's point of view, the viability of an export-led development strategy based on the assembly industry depends on the extent to which the industry can create beneficial links with the host economy in addition to the direct employment and foreign exchange generated. Probably the single most important link is known as "backward linkages" (Hirschman 1958); that is, the degree to which national inputs are used in the production process.[21] The nature of assembly industry—based as it is on the importation of components, the use of low wage labor to perform the assembly "service," and the reexport of the final products—has justified its being dubbed an "enclave" in much of the literature (Kindleberger 1968).[22]

Nevertheless, the four Asian tigers have used assembly industry as a springboard to broader and deeper industrialization. Spinanger's calculations (Spinanger 1984) of imported versus domestic inputs among assembly plants in Asian export-processing zones show graphically the tremendous rise in the percentage of domestic inputs for South Korea and Taiwan (see Figure 1): The proportion of domestic inputs among assembly plants in export-processing zones rose from 13 percent in 1972 to 32 percent in 1977 for South Korea and from 5 percent in 1967 to 27 percent in 1978 for Taiwan. Singapore's proportion of domestic inputs remained rather flat but very high:[23] 40 percent in 1972, peaking at 45 percent in 1977, followed by 43 percent in 1979.[24] While comparable figures are not available for Hong Kong, Henderson (1989: 140–141) reports the emergence of seven locally owned semiconductor manufacturers in Hong Kong that supply consumer electronics plants with subassemblies.

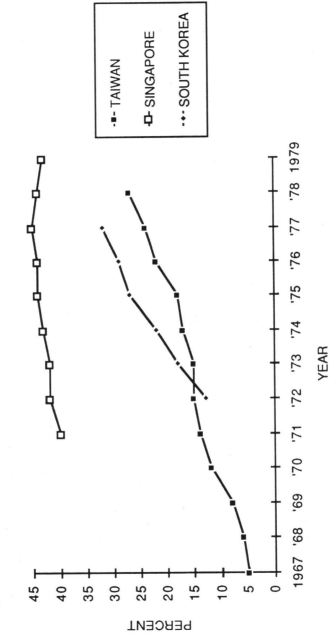

Figure 1. Growth of Domestic Inputs in Asian Assembly Manufacturing (as percent of total inputs)

Source: Compiled from Spinanger (1984: 79), using data provided by export-processing zones (three-year floating averages used; Singapore data include purchases from other EPZ firms in the country as domestic inputs).

Not only have the four newly industrializing countries of Asia been able to develop domestic suppliers for the foreign assembly plants, they have created some domestic industries that are competitive with the foreign firms. In Taiwan, for example, foreign electronics assembly helped spawn a domestic electronics industry making computer clones for the world market (Spinanger 1984: 84). Taiwan is also producing its own telecommunications equipment, precision machinery, optical instruments, and biotechnology. South Korea is well known for its production of consumer durables for the international market. Hong Kong's locally owned semiconductor firms have moved beyond subcontract assembly into advanced circuit testing and wafer manufacturing (Henderson 1989: 140–141).

With the local supplier base growing and wages rising (see Table 7), assembly plants in all four countries have been upgrading to higher technology products and processes in which labor costs comprise just a small part (Henderson 1989: 126).[25] This trend is not restricted to electronics: Some textile and apparel assembly plants have invested in automated equipment, while others are moving production to cheaper labor locations.[26] Currie describes her case study of a Hong Kong textile firm that was doing both: automating its production in Singapore and Hong Kong (not so much to reduce labor costs as to improve quality control) while at the same time shifting some production to Malaysia (the firm also tried manufacturing in the United States, but found the labor force "insufficiently versatile") (Currie 1984: 30). Assembly industry in the Asian tigers has become a much higher value-added activity, qualitatively different from the original labor intensive assembly.

A number of scholars have concluded—sometimes reluctantly—that while assembly industry in the Asian tigers started off as typical enclaves, it eventually established backward linkages to the firms in the host country (see Schive 1988). These "success stories" have prompted some economists to generalize a pattern: " 'First-stage' international sourcing within a divisible production process—such as the location of semiconductor or television assembly in a developing country—then gives rise to 'second-stage' international sourcing—the transfer to the developing country of input production as well" (Lim and Pang 1982: 591).

In most other countries with export processing, however, domestic linkages have remained small, including in other Asian countries (see Table 8).[27] Mexico's assembly industry shows no trend toward increasing its current 1.5 percent share of domestic content (see chapter 3). In the Dominican Republic, which has overtaken

Table 7 *The Growth of Manufacturing Wages in the Asian "Tigers" (average monthly industrial wages per worker in U.S. dollars)*

	1964	1988
Asian "tigers"		
South Korea[a]	$302	$633
Taiwan[a]	325	598
Singapore[a]	416	547
Hong Kong[a]	363	544
Other Asian Countries		
Thailand	n.a.	80
Philippines	n.a.	75
Malaysia	n.a.	55
Indonesia	n.a.	55
China[b]	n.a.	40

Source: Compiled from Lee (1989: 78) and Yang (1989: 45).
[a]Includes bonuses and overtime.
[b]Excludes state subsidies.

Haiti as the leading export-processing country in the Caribbean, the use of local inputs also remains very small (Thoumi 1988).

Historical Factors

What explains the ability of the four Asian tigers to multiply their linkages from assembly industry during the 1970s? An important part of the explanation lies in unique or unreplicable historical factors: The first factor is the colonial heritage. By World War II Japanese colonial rule in Taiwan and Korea—unlike U.S., British, or Spanish domination in Latin America—had left a substantial manufacturing infrastructure (see above). The Japanese had spun off light industries for which they no longer perceived a comparative advantage. British colonial rule in Singapore and Hong Kong had left an export-oriented infrastructure of transportation, communications, and financial services.

The second important historical factor for all but Singapore was the influx of entrepreneurs, professionals, and skilled workers fleeing Communist upheavals in China and North Korea. This selective migration spurred the formation of local industrial capital, management, and labor force in South Korea, Taiwan, and Hong Kong.

Third, massive U.S. foreign aid helped finance local industrial development. From 1946 to 1978, South Korea alone received nearly $6 billion in U.S. economic grants and loans, compared to less than $15 billion for all of Latin America during the same years (Cumings 1984: 24). U.S. military aid to Taiwan and South Korea from 1955 (i.e., after the Korean War) to 1978 surpassed $9 billion, while all of Latin America and Africa together received $3.2 billion (Cumings 1984: 24).

Finally, there was little threat of U.S. protectionism to thwart the Asian tigers' export growth in the late sixties. Beginning in the early 1970s, however, there was growing concern in the United States about foreign countries—especially newly industrializing countries—subsidizing their exports and protecting their domestic markets. In the mid-seventies the United States began to apply "orderly marketing agreements" and "voluntary export restraints," which took on the nature of protective tariffs and quotas (Fajnzylber 1981: 129).

Role of the State

Latin American countries trying to get on the export-led bandwagon face major obstacles: a detrimental legacy of social relations accompanying import substitution (see above), increased protectionism by the advanced countries, and not just a lack of financial capital but massive foreign debt. Despite the differing historical conditions that make an easy transfer of the Asian "lessons" to Latin America impossible, there were some public policies the Asian four pursued to build upon their assembly industry that perhaps have some possibility of replicability in Mexico and other Latin American countries today.

First, all four countries used assembly manufacturing as a stepping stone—a transitory device—toward a full export-led industrialization. In three of the four—Taiwan, Korea, and Singapore—export processing was part of a shift in national commitment from an inward-oriented development strategy to an outward-oriented one. None of the four adopted export processing primarily as a regional development strategy. Those that at first confined their export processing to specified zones later began to offer nationwide incentives to foreign investors. They began to allow custom-free treatment even to firms that sold part of their product on the domestic market, just to gain access to more foreign exchange and technology (Currie 1984). Victor Sit (1988: 668) describes this trend for Taiwan: "With the rapid expansion of its exporting sector and the gradual creation

Table 8 *Domestic Material Content in Assembly Manufacturing for Selected Countries (percentage of total inputs)*

	Percentage Domestic Content
Mexico (1979)	2%
Malaysia (1978)	3
Sri Lanka (1980)	3
Singapore (1979)[a]	42
South Korea (1977)	33
Taiwan (1978)	27

Source: Compiled from Currie (1984: 38), for first three, and table 7 above for last three countries.

[a]Includes purchases from other firms in export-processing zones.

of numerous well-planned industrial areas and districts throughout the island, the significance of the EPZs in Taiwan's overall export economy . . . declined. . . . The three EPZs have been more or less stagnant since 1976, and the industrial products exported from them are still highly biased toward labor-intensive types, reflecting Taiwan's former comparative advantage in cheap labor." Similarly, the major export-processing zone in South Korea (Masan Free Export Zone), set up near Seoul in 1970, had become stagnant by 1976. "As in Taiwan, the rising overall wage level and the general success of export-oriented industrialization have made new EPZs in South Korea unnecessary" (Sit 1988: 668).

Second, the governments of Korea, Taiwan, and Singapore promoted foreign assembly industry in the context of strong government guidance of the economy aimed at protecting and developing the domestic industries that would both supply the assembly plants and also create the basis for a broader-based export-oriented industrialization using domestic firms and technology. The Korean government, for example, has selected different sectors to protect and develop in each of its five-year development plans since 1962. Through strong central control of financial capital, the Korean government collaborates very closely with the private sector (Fajnzylber 1981: p. 122). The government of Singapore also plays a strong role in guiding the industrialization process. With a small domestic private sector, however, Singapore's government opted to develop domestic industry largely through state-owned enterprises and joint ventures. In 1983 the government had at least partial interest in 450 enterprises, sixty-five of which were in manufacturing (Krause 1987: 117).

The governments of Taiwan, Korea, and Singapore have also pressured private manufacturers to upgrade their technology and directly intervened in capital markets to influence the technology. The governments of both Singapore and Taiwan have created science parks, special zones providing financial incentives to foreign and domestic firms—regardless of market orientation—that invest in R&D in order to promote greater technology transfer and domestic technology development.[28] Even the government of Hong Kong supports a manufacturing design center (the Hong Kong Productivity Center), including a semiconductor design facility. The public education system in Hong Kong has also provided the engineers and technicians which allow the advanced testing facilities, wafer fabrication plants, and at least low-level R&D to operate (Henderson 1989: 141).

Third, the Asian tigers have been rather successful at utilizing foreign investment to achieve national objectives. The governments of Korea, Taiwan, and Hong Kong have kept direct foreign investment to a small role, preferring foreign financial capital (particularly long-term loans).[29] In 1978, foreign capital's share of manufactured exports varied between 10 and 20 percent in Hong Kong, Taiwan, and South Korea, compared to 25 to 40 percent in Latin America (Fajnzylber 1981: 125). Even in Singapore, where foreign capital accounted for over 80 percent of manufactured exports in 1978 (Koh 1987: 25), the government guides foreign investment by tying incentives to particular behaviors such as investing in priority sectors, upgrading capital intensivity, or undertaking on-site R&D.

Thus, the Asian experience shows that export-led industrialization does not require a small role for the state, an end to import substitution, or total submission to foreign capital. In other words, to pursue a role in the new global economy, Third World countries need not convert themselves into "passive objects of international market forces" (Fajnzylber 1981: 122). On the contrary, to forge domestic linkages from foreign assembly industry and lay the basis for a full-fledged export-oriented industrialization, the Asian tigers (at least three out of four) did quite the opposite: maintained a central role for the state in guiding the economy, pursued a deepening of import substitution, and kept foreign capital within the boundaries of national interest.

New Trends

Social Unrest in the Asian Tigers

There are no "happily ever after" stories in the dialectical play of history. The main factor contributing to the stable growth of export-oriented industrialization in the four Asian tigers may have become the undoing of that stability: the "disciplining" of the labor force. Social unrest in the Asian tigers is now rampant. The labor force is no longer passive. Even in comparatively tame Hong Kong, popular pressure on the government since 1982 has risen to an "unprecedented level" (Lo, 1988: 613). In South Korea, where wage increases now far outstrip productivity increases, student and labor uprisings in the late 1980s eroded the government's long-standing autonomy from social pressure, forcing President Roh Tae-Woo into "an extremely delicate balancing act" (Neff and Nakarmi 1989: 39). In Taiwan the lifting of martial law in mid-1987 unleashed labor strife in the textile, electronics, auto, and paper industries. Labor shortages have become a problem, particularly in lower wage industries, in Hong Kong, Taiwan, and Singapore (Yang and Nakarmi 1989: 46). The ruling party in Korea is reportedly hoping for a strong recession to put labor back in its place, since the government has been unable to do so (Neff and Nakarmi 1989: 39).

China's Entry into the Global Assembly Industry

With labor unrest, wages, and labor shortages mounting in the four Asian tigers, the People's Republic of China—with the lowest wages in East Asia, no strikes, and a potentially huge internal market— has become attractive to foreign investors. The Chinese government shifted from an internally oriented development strategy to an externally oriented one in 1978. In the context of this "open door" policy, the government opted to concentrate foreign investment along the isolated and little developed southern coast.

The government established four Special Economic Zones in this region, in which the normal central controls over capital, production, pricing, and markets would be suspended and tax incentives granted. Through joint ventures with foreign investors, the government expected technology, managerial skills, and worker skills to flow into China, as well as capital. Foreign investors, on the other hand, saw these zones not only as providing access to inexpensive Chinese labor (see Table 7), but also access to the Chinese market. The most attractive zone to foreign capital (mainly from Hong Kong, Japan, and the United States) has been Shenzhen, a rural area contiguous to Hong Kong.[30]

China's mixed experience with the Shenzhen Special Economic Zone has been instructive. Sklair reports that Shenzhen has been successful not just in luring foreign assembly plants interested in low cost labor but in developing the infrastructure of the region, creating some backward linkages with the rest of the economy (primarily with Chinese-made steel and electronics components) and upgrading workers' skills:

> Investments in infrastructure (roads, factories, commercial, tourist, and residential construction, telecommunications, energy) have transformed the area out of all recognition. . . . The technicians and managers from Hong Kong, Japan, Europe, and the U.S. are very much encouraged to pass on their skills and to some extent their techniques to the local Chinese, at all levels. Large numbers of Chinese from other parts of the country have come to Shenzhen to put their skills to use and to upgrade these skills through contact with the new industries. . . . The creation of the SEZ has stimulated the establishment of a new university at Shenzhen, geared to the practical needs of the zone. (Sklair 1986: 8–9)

On the other hand, Chu (1987: 83) reports that Shenzhen turned into "a giant marketplace for foreign-made consumer goods and illegal dealings in foreign exchange." The foreign investment has been primarily in lucrative real estate development (catching pent-up Hong Kong demand for land) rather than factories, and most of the factories have been traditional labor intensive assembly plants. After a decade of experience with the "open door," China has not been able to follow the path of the four tigers.

The Search for Manufactured Exports in Latin America

Faced with a shortage of foreign exchange, more Latin American countries adopted export-oriented strategies during the 1980s, often citing the Asian tigers as their model. "Nontraditional" exports, particularly manufactured ones, became the fashionable target. Within this spreading export orientation, only Mexico and the Caribbean have given an important role to assembly industry, although Brazil passed legislation authorizing new export-processing zones in 1987 (Inter-American Development Bank 1988: 66).

In the mid-1980s, a number of Caribbean countries opted for a full-fledged export-oriented development strategy using assembly industry. Shrinking quotas on traditional agricultural and mineral exports spurred this strategy shift, as did the creation of the Caribbean Basin Initiative[31] by the United States and the parallel agreements with Canada and the European Community. New expressions of interest from Hong Kong, Taiwanese, and Korean assembly firms fleeing import quotas also buoyed Caribbean interest in the strategy shift.[32]

The Dominican Republic has been the most successful Caribbean country to make the policy switch. To lower the cost of exports—and the wages that go into them—the government devalued the currency and opened six new export-processing zones between 1988 and 1989, for a total of thirteen.[33] Total direct employment in export processing expanded from 60,000 to 90,000 in that year. In 1989 the government passed a law to ease the red tape for assembly plant investors. The zones now account for over half of all manufacturing jobs, one-third of the Dominican Republic's exports, 25 percent of local value added, and over 8 percent of national employment. Most zone operations remain concentrated in low technology, labor intensive assembly—apparel, electronics, and footwear—although recent arrivals have included data entry and computer graphics. Ninety percent of the assembly plants are foreign-owned, even though small local investors are now getting more involved in textile operations. The zones remain "little islands of prosperity on this economically troubled island," with "no prospects for appreciable linkages," according to a 1989 assessment by the Caribbean Basin Initiative Office (U.S. Department of Commerce, unclassified incoming telegram, March 1989).

Barbados similarly rejected import substitution in its 1983–1987 development plan and concentrated its efforts on attracting assembly industry. Electronic component assembly multiplied five fold from 1981 to 1984, accounting for half the island's total exports in 1984 (Long 1986: 38). Jamaica experienced an even more abrupt policy turnaround: During the socialist government of the 1970s foreign capital was not encouraged, but in the 1980s the Seaga government made export-led industrialization the cornerstone of the country's economic development strategy. Devaluations made the Jamaican labor costs among the lowest in the Caribbean. Assembly exports from the Kingston Free Zone multiplied more than ten times between 1980 and 1984, mostly in textiles and garments. Ninety percent of all the assembly plants are foreign-owned, half from Hong Kong and half from the United States (Long 1986).

In 1980 Trinidad and Tobago also shifted to an export-led strategy, but one based on its natural resources rather than its inexpensive labor. The government opened the Point Lisas Industrial Estate, offering the usual import duty exemptions on raw materials and machinery. But it pursued export-oriented chemical and steel industries rather than traditional assembly. At Point Lisas, small locally owned firms in fertilizers, plastics, and sports equipment predominate in number. They are labor intensive with simple technology. The large firms, however, account for most of the employment. The huge capital intensive firms in petrochemicals, iron, and steel account for the bulk of the employment. They make fertilizer, nitrogen, ammonia, methanol, urea, and steel for the export market. Over half the large firms are totally state owned, a third are joint ventures between the state and foreign corporations (with 51 percent state capital), and the remainder are totally foreign-owned. Many of the smaller firms are actually spin-offs of the large ones, having been created under licensing arrangements and turn-key contracts with the foreign corporations. There are no textile and electronic firms at Point Lisas. While Point Lisas accounts for less than 1 percent of total national employment, its exports have overtaken sugar as the second largest source of foreign exchange after mineral fuel lubricants (Long 1986).

Mexico, too, entered a new phase of its assembly industry in the 1980s. The industry grew beyond a regional development strategy to gain national importance after the government adopted a full-fledged export-led strategy in 1982. Two significant trends altered the nature of assembly industry in Mexico during the 1980s: the rise of higher value-added manufacturing and the adoption of flexible manufacturing methods in a significant portion of the maquiladoras (see chapter 4). Yet Mexico has not been able to take much advantage of these trends to create local supplier linkages. Like China after ten years, Mexico after twenty-five years has not been able to follow the path of the Asian tigers.

Policy Implications for Mexico

Some of the factors giving rise to the Asian success stories are historically unique and out of Mexico's control to replicate, including massive foreign aid from the United States, selective immigration of entrepreneurs and skilled workers, and an absence of U.S. protectionism. It is historically too late for Mexico to change some factors: Mexico already started out using the assembly industry as an isolated regional development program, rather than as part of a national strategy aimed at export-led development. Mexico already inherited a legacy of organized labor, middle-class, and popular demands that the government during import substitution could not ignore.

Nevertheless, Mexico has probably the most striking similarity to the Asian cases of any Latin American country: a strong, authoritarian state that has been able to channel popular demands through a corporatist political system so as not to threaten the state's autonomy. The Mexican state also was able to guide the country's import substitution process to a much deeper level of industrialization than in most Latin American countries (except Brazil). Moreover, in the 1980s Mexico has gone far in recreating two of the key conditions responsible for the Asian success stories: first, a total national commitment to export-led development; and second, a firm hand in disciplining labor, rolling back many of its gains from the period of import substitution. The government has had amazing success so far in lowering real wage levels since 1982 without provoking threatening upheavals. Part of this success is due to the fact that the Mexican labor force still has some options: migrate to the United States or withdraw from the formal labor force. This latter option is a latent threat to the assembly industry, which is still largely a female labor force. If austerity measures make daily life too costly and assembly wages do not improve, maquiladora workers may find family survival requires them to return to unpaid labor in the home or informal sector work to try to reduce the cost of living for the family.

What is the main lesson from the Asian tigers for Mexico? A successful export-oriented development strategy does not require increasing free trade or laissez-faire policies. The cases of South Korea, Taiwan, and Singapore shows that a strong state is useful to protect domestic industries that supply the export manufacturers and to channel foreign investment into the desired sectors and technologies. Without state guidance to ensure local linkages from its manufactured exports, the free trade agreement with the United States could mean simply the further maquilization of Mexico's manufacturing industry. Only with concerted state action can the Mexican government's export-led strategy lead to a comparative advantage beyond that of cheap labor. Without it, the maquiladora industry will remain primarily an enclave.

Mexico faces new conditions in the changing global economy not encountered by the Asian tigers that could be a help or a hindrance to export-led industrialization. Many leading-edge multinational corporations have gone beyond large scale mass production methods to adopt flexible manufacturing techniques. Mexico's assembly workers have shown willingness and ability to adopt the new shop floor methods of flexible manufacturing (see chapter 4). These new methods involving labor-management cooperation have generated resistance among U.S. unions.[34] Taiwanese workers are reportedly too accustomed to authoritarian militaristic discipline on the factory floor to be able to participate freely in labor-management quality circles.[35] Foreign factory managers in China have found it hard to increase productivity and quality standards among workers accustomed to guaranteed jobs in state-owned factories (Chu 1987). In Latin America, Caribbean export manufacturing remains concentrated in routine assembly and is highly dependent on U.S. quotas and tax incentives. Thus Mexico may be left with a rich opportunity to garner a larger role in leading-edge flexible manufacturing for export. However, initial evidence indicates that it may be even more difficult for Mexico to create local linkages from flexible manufacturing than from more traditional industry (chapter 4).

Mexico needs to take greater advantage of its foreign assembly industry by looking at how the Asian tigers used strong state control to forge local linkages from assembly industry and to upgrade the technology to more capital intensive methods and eventually local R&D. In this light, maquiladoras should be seen as a transitory measure—by choice and necessity—in an export-led strategy that can lead to a comparative advantage beyond that of cheap labor.

3. The Rise of the New Maquiladoras

Origins of the Maquiladora Industry

From the 1950s through the 1970s Mexico's economic development strategy was based on import substitution—the developmentalist idea that the state must actively foster industrial development by building the necessary physical infrastructure, protecting infant domestic industries from foreign competition, and expanding the internal market through populist reforms. Mexico was one of the most successful countries of Latin America in pursuing import substitution: Per capita income rose; a large, educated middle class developed; and urban industrial growth flourished.

Not all the regions of Mexico shared in the prosperity of import substitution. One of those excluded was the northern border region, whose market was saturated by easily available American-made goods. In 1961 President López Mateos asked the leading businessman from Juárez, Antonio Bermúdez, to head up the Programa Nacional Fronterizo (PRONAF) to revitalize the border cities. The approach Bermúdez took was fully consistent with the leading import substitution model of the day: Find ways to provide Mexican-made goods to the border market so that the demand would not be satisfied across the border with U.S. goods. However, PRONAF's "buy Mexico" campaign was largely a failure and the industrial parks that Bermúdez envisioned filled with Mexican factories producing for the border market never materialized. Adding to the need for jobs in the border region, in 1964 the United States dismantled the bracero program, a twenty-two-year-old agreement between the U.S. and Mexican governments that had legalized the flow of over four million Mexican migrant farmworkers to the United States (Sklair 1989: 28–30).

That same year the minister of Industry and Commerce under President Díaz Ordaz toured the Far East, where he saw U.S. corporations rapidly setting up assembly plants (see chapter 2). A year later, the minister announced a similar program for Mexico's border region, calling it the Border Industrialization Program.[1] The BIP allowed foreign and Mexican investors to temporarily import duty-free all the inputs, machinery, and replacement parts needed for assembly as long as the investors bought a bond that would ensure their eventual reexportation. The government referred to those plants setting up under the BIP as *maquiladoras*.[2]

The Border Industrialization Program provided a new source of demand for Bermúdez' industrial parks: maquiladoras. While inconsistent with his vision of domestic industry, the BIP did promise to benefit the local business class through industrial land development. The Bermúdez family, in fact, became the prime supporter of the maquiladora industry along the border and the major industrial park developer in Juárez.

Legal Framework

A precise legal framework for the maquiladora industry was not announced until 1971, when there were already more than two hundred maquiladoras employing about 30,000 workers (Sklair 1989: 45). The 1971 regulations permit full foreign ownership of maquiladoras, a sharp contrast to the existing restriction on firms producing for the internal market to 49 percent foreign ownership. The foreign (usually U.S.) corporation that wishes to set up its own maquiladora has two choices. One is to set up a wholly owned Mexican subsidiary of the parent company. The other is to establish a joint venture with a Mexican partner (Tarbox 1986: 118).[3] Both these arrangements result in a captive producer; that is, a maquiladora producing solely—or almost solely—for its parent company.

Another arrangement is the shelter operation in which a foreign company or individual subcontracts with a Mexican company to assemble the goods and handle all the paperwork involving Mexican customs laws. The Mexican company is typically a full-time shelter operation, often with multiple foreign clients. This alternative is used primarily by small foreign companies who do not wish to undertake the risk or investment required in setting up their own Mexican corporation. A Mexican company producing for the internal market that has idle capacity can also assemble goods for foreign clients as a maquiladora shelter operation.

There are three ways of entering the maquiladora business for a Mexican company that produces for the internal market but wants access to the foreign assembly market: as a partner in a joint venture with a foreign corporation, having its own wholly owned subsidiary registered as a maquiladora, or as a shelter operation using excess capacity.[4] The latter is more frequent in the interior, as we shall see below. Some Mexican firms find it advantageous to stay registered as a maquiladora even if they no longer do assembly work for foreign clients because they can leave imported equipment and machinery in-bond without paying import duties on them.

The 1971 regulations created much red tape to become a maquiladora. Once the Mexican corporation was formed, the investors had to register with the Ministry of Finance, the General Bureau of Statistics, and the Mexican Social Security Institute. Then they submitted their maquiladora application and requests for in-bond status to the Ministry of Industry and Commerce in Mexico City. The 1971 regulations restricted maquiladoras to the twenty-kilometer strip parallel to the international border (however, exceptions were granted in some interior locations, such as Guadalajara).

Existing U.S. tariff laws provided an added incentive for maquiladoras beyond that of the Mexican duty exemptions and the cheap labor. Items 806.30 and 807.00 of the U.S. Tariff Schedules (hereafter 806/807) exempt from U.S. customs duties the portion of the reimported article's value that is of U.S. origin. Item 806 allows metal articles that are manufactured in the United States, assembled abroad, and returned to the United States for further processing to be imported duty-free except on the value of the foreign processing. Item 807, of more relevance to the maquiladoras, allows fabricated components made in the United States to be reimported duty-free if they are assembled abroad into either intermediate or final goods. If value-added processing other than assembly (i.e., manufacturing) is done abroad, the components lose their 807 tax exemption.

In 1976 the U.S. government created another tax break that could be enjoyed by some maquiladoras. The United States joined twenty-two other countries in the Generalized System of Preferences program. The GSP had been started by industrialized nations in the 1960s as a temporary measure to give developing countries preferential tariff treatment of their manufactured exports until they became fully competitive with developed nations. Responding to requests from participating developing country governments, producers, or importers, the GSP subcommittee designates articles to receive duty-free treatment if certain conditions are met. For the maquiladoras, 35 percent of the value of the goods must be added in Mexico. Labor as well as domestically manufactured inputs, fuels, and electricity can be counted in the 35 percent (Schwartz 1987: 10–11).[5]

The First Phase: 1965–1982

The early maquiladoras gave rise to the industry's image as exploitative fly-by-night sweatshops taking advantage of young female workers. The image found fertile ground in the anti-imperialist anti-American sentiment that was common in the period of import substitution (Bustamante 1975). Mexico's last populist president of the era, Echeverría, introduced a federal labor law in 1970 that provided significant improvements for maquiladora workers, as well as other blue-collar workers. They were given mandatory paid vacations and Christmas bonuses; mandatory training and recreation programs; death, termination, and retirement benefits to be paid by the employer; employer-provided housing assistance; and a guarantee of the minimum wage for apprenticeships abolished. Maquiladoras with more than one hundred employees had to introduce these changes within three years (Sklair 1989: 55).

Despite these gains, labor force militancy increased in the early 1970s (Baird and McCaughan 1975) as the government-affiliated labor union (CTM) lost control of the workers. Prompted by the labor demands and an overvalued peso, maquiladora wages rose to the point where they were no longer competitive with Asia and the Caribbean. Many maquiladoras threatened to leave. However, it took the U.S. recession of 1973–74 to make the threats good: In 1974 and 1975 maquiladora employment and number of plants actually dropped (INEGI 1983).

Both government and labor reacted with a more conciliatory attitude toward the maquiladoras. CTM regained control of the workers, who were scared of losing their jobs. President López Portillo devalued the peso in 1976 and took a tougher stand against labor, allowing the maquiladoras more latitude with respect to the workers. Inefficient workers could be fired without severance pay; the thirty-day probationary period at below minimum wage was extended to ninety days; and employer contributions to the social security fund were reduced. Also, López Portillo introduced a new promotional program for the maquiladora industry, called the Alliance for Production, which reduced the red tape required in establishing a maquiladora and financed the construction of industrial parks and infrastructure in the border cities (Sklair 1989: 62–63).

Growth picked up for a few more years again in the maquiladora industry after the devaluation of 1976 and the U.S. boom of 1977, but again the government gave in to demands for real increases in the minimum wage. While the hourly rate in the maquiladoras was

57 cents in 1976 (about half that before the devaluation), by 1980 it was up to 89 cents. In 1981 it was raised to $1.12 and raised again in 1982 to $1.53 (Sklair 1989: 65). Starting in 1980–81 maquiladora plants and employment again declined, with a loss of nearly four thousand jobs between 1981 and 1982. Not only had real minimum wage rates almost tripled in five years, the wages were again uncompetitive with Asia. López Portillo devalued the peso just before leaving office in 1982, thereby cutting real wages in half (Sklair 1989: 65–67).

The Second Phase: Since 1982

If there is one year that marks a major turning point in the maquiladora industry it is 1982.[6] Before that, the maquiladora industry was primarily just a regional development program, an anomaly in the prevailing import substitution strategy. After that, it became a mainstay of the government's export-oriented development strategy. President Miguel de la Madrid came in to office with a strongly neoliberal platform: join GATT and reduce protectionist tariffs, make it easier for foreign investment to operate in Mexico, cut public spending, reduce wages and control inflation, and sell off state enterprises. De la Madrid continued to devalue the peso, and real wages declined 40 percent in his term of office.

De la Madrid declared the maquiladora industry a priority sector for the economy (*Business Mexico* [February 1986]: 86–87, cited in Sklair 1989). He wanted to promote the industry primarily as a source of foreign exchange and jobs, but also as a way of catalyzing endogenous industrial development (see Villarreal Arrambide 1986). In 1983 de la Madrid brought forth a new legal decree for the maquiladora industry that reflected both goals. It promoted the industry by making it even easier to set up and operate a maquiladora. A single administrative organ was set up to oversee the industry, and its administration was decentralized out of Mexico City to the border states and other maquiladora locations. The 1983 decree also allowed maquiladoras to apply for permission to sell up to 20 percent of their production in Mexico if there were no competing Mexican goods available. To promote the integration of the maquiladora industry with endogenous industry, the decree allowed maquiladoras to be located virtually anywhere except Mexico City and encouraged maquiladoras to locate in the less developed parts of Mexico. The decree also exhorted them—but with no real sticks or carrots—to buy more inputs from domestic suppliers and to transfer technology to them. With the devaluations and official encouragement, the maquiladora industry boomed during the de la Madrid administration, becoming the largest source of foreign exchange after petroleum and before tourism.

Also during de la Madrid's term, two new legal alternatives to maquiladora status were added to make it easier for Mexican firms to get involved in export processing: PITEX (Programa para la Importación Temporal para Exportación) and ALTEX (Programa para las Industrias Altamente Exportadoras). Established in 1985 (*Diario Oficial*, May 9, 1985, pp. 6–8), the new options permit the same duty-free treatment of temporary in-bond imports of inputs and machinery as does the maquiladora regimen. Large firms with over $5 million in annual sales could qualify for PITEX if they exported as little as 10 percent of gross sales. Small firms could qualify for ALTEX if they exported at least 50 percent of their output.

President Salinas de Gortari continued the neoliberal strategy of promoting manufactured exports, reducing wages and inflation, privatizing state enterprises, lowering tariffs and easing restrictions on foreign capital. The Foreign Investment Regulation of May 1989 granted some of the benefits of being a foreign-owned maquiladora to foreign firms that do not register as maquiladoras. For example, the regulation granted unrestricted foreign ownership of export manufacturing outside the maquiladora industry, heretofore a benefit reserved almost exclusively for maquiladoras. In addition, the regulation expanded eligibility for the PITEX and ALTEX programs to include companies with greater than 50 percent foreign ownership. Thus, foreign companies that would have become maquiladoras now have the option of registering under PITEX or ALTEX and gaining the same in-bond incentives. Since the 1989 regulation also permitted maquiladoras to enter more freely into the domestic market, the choice between PITEX/ALTEX and maquiladora status has boiled down to a technical decision weighing the subtle and complicated differences in foreign exchange requirements and tax treatment.[7] The 1989 regulation also made it easier for foreign maquiladoras to own real property along the coastal and border zones.

To further promote export processing President Salinas put forth a new maquiladora decree in December 1989. The decree authorizes a one-stop permitting procedure for maquiladoras at the regional offices of the Secretariat of Commerce and Industrial Development (SECOFI) and simplifies customs administration. Duty-free status is extended to service companies supplying maquiladoras and to subcontractors of maquiladoras. Mexican suppliers of maquiladoras are authorized a 100 percent exemption from the value-added tax. Maquiladoras may sell up to 50 percent of their output in Mexico, provided duties on imported inputs are paid. The decree also states the government's commitment to develop new zones for the maquiladora industry in the interior in order to better integrate the industry with domestic suppliers. In sum, the decree emphasizes that the maquiladora industry continues to be a "priority activity" within Mexico's development strategy.

The New Maquiladoras

What was once an anomalous export-oriented regional development program in the context of a protected internal market is now a priority component of a national development strategy aimed at the external market. But it is not just the national development strategy that has changed. The nature of the maquiladora industry itself has changed since 1982. The most obvious change is the take-off in growth starting in 1982 (see Figure 2), reflecting the devaluations that made maquiladora wages more attractive than Asian wages. But the big changes are far more than quantitative. There are important qualitative changes in the very work process of the maquiladora plants that reflect the changing strategies of both foreign and domestic capital in response to the changing global economy. While the next few chapters explore these changing strategies and their motivations in depth, I wish to set the stage here with some general indicators of these deep-seated changes.

First, the maquiladora industry is no longer simply low productivity, labor intensive assembly activity. Worker productivity has increased; the production process is more capital intensive; and many maquiladoras now do actual manufacturing, along with assembly. In other words, they add value to the product by transforming components, not just assembling them. A good indicator of increasing capital intensiveness is the proportion of labor costs to total operating costs. Table 9 shows a noticeable drop in this ratio after 1981. The rise of manufacturing in the maquiladora industry is also associated with the decline in the use of female line workers, who are associated primarily with assembly activity. Table 9 shows a distinct drop in the percentage of female line workers after 1982. Table 9 also shows how worker productivity, measured as value added per worker in constant pesos, is higher after 1981 than before. This trend is corroborated by the rise in the use of skilled workers and in the growth of average plant size after 1981. Even with rising productivity per worker, however, the return to labor in the form

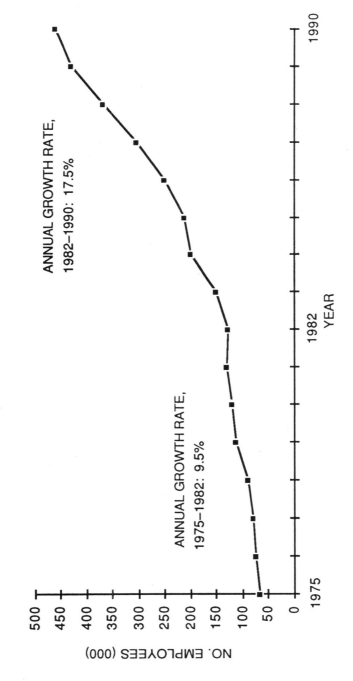

Figure 2. Employment in the Maquiladora Industry, 1975–1990

ANNUAL GROWTH RATE,
1982–1990: 17.5%

ANNUAL GROWTH RATE,
1975–1982: 9.5%

NO. EMPLOYEES (000)

500
450
400
350
300
250
200
150
100
50
0

1975   1982   1990
            YEAR

Source: INEGI, various years.

Table 9 *Changing Characteristics of the Maquiladoras, 1975–1990*

	Value added per worker (000,000 pesos)[a]	Labor costs as percent of total operating costs[b] %	Labor costs as percent of value added %	Percent skilled workers %	Percent female workers[c] %	Average size of plant (no. workers)[d]
1975	196	19		9	78	148
1976	198	19	61	9	79	166
1977	189	18	64	9	78	177
1978	197	17	60	9	77	198
1979	197	17	58	9	77	206
1980	174	18	59	10	77	193
1981	175	19	61	10	77	216
Average '75–'81	189	18	60	9	78	186
1982	211	16	53	11	77	217
1983	200	11	47	12	74	251
1984	193	12	52	12	71	297
1985	207	13	52	13	69	279
1986	243	10	45	13	68	281
1987	224	11	46	13	66	271
1988	215	11	49	13	63	265
1989	218	12	51	13	61	261
1990	243	13	51		61	238
Average '82–'90	217	12	50	13	68	262

Source: INEGI (1988, 1989, 1990, 1991).

[a]Constant pesos of 1980, using "Indices de Precios Implicitos" from *Sistemas de Cuentas Nacionales de México: Cuentas de Producción,* INEGI, various years. Workers defined as unskilled line workers. Value added includes domestic content.

[b]Calculated as total remunerations divided by the sum of domestic value added plus imported inputs.

[c]Line workers.

Table 10 *The Changing Sectoral Composition of the
Maquiladora Industry, 1979–1990*

	Percentage distribution of total employment		
	1979	1982	1990
Transportation equipment	4.5	9.7	21.5
Electric and electronic equipment	25.7	26.1	11.6
Electric and electronic materials	31.2	32.3	25.3
All other	38.5	32.0	41.6
TOTAL	100.0 %	100.0 %	100.0 %

Source: INEGI (1989, 1990, 1991).

of wages, salaries, and benefits has gone down during the 1980s.
Table 9 shows that remunerations as a share of value added declined sharply after 1981. This trend reflects the weakened strength
of labor in the neoliberal climate, compared to the populist days of
import substitution.

The sectoral composition of the maquiladora industry has also
changed dramatically. This change in part explains the rise of manufacturing, productivity, and use of men in the labor force. Table
10 shows the dramatic rise of transportation equipment—primarily
automobile subassemblies—since 1982 at the expense of electric and
electronic equipment and materials.[8]

The Growth of the Interior Maquiladoras

The story of the new maquiladoras is to some degree the story of
the rise of the interior maquiladoras. A few interior maquiladoras
were established in the late sixties and early seventies—in Chihuahua City (230 miles from Juárez), Mérida in the Yucatán, Zar-
agoza (50 miles from the Texas border town of Eagle Pass), and
Guadalajara, and later in Torreón, near Mexico City. Through the
latter 1970s interior maquiladoras hovered at about 10 percent of
the total (see Table 11). Since 1983 maquiladoras in the interior have
grown more rapidly than at the border (see Table 11), nearly dou-
bling the percent of the labor force to almost 20 percent between
1983 and 1988.

Since the late 1970s, the Mexican government has sought to de-
centralize maquiladora activity, in part to dilute the growing political strength of the border region and its opposition party (PAN),
in part to relieve infrastructure pressure in the border cities, in part

to stimulate lagging regions, and in part to integrate maquiladora development more closely with domestic producers. President López Portillo's industrial development plan of 1979 encouraged maquiladoras to move to less developed areas such as the Yucatán and Oaxaca. De la Madrid's maquiladora decree of 1983 actually gave some concrete incentives to locate in underdeveloped interior locations: 40 percent of output could be sold on the domestic market, as opposed to 20 percent for maquiladoras elsewhere. The Salinas government has promoted interior maquiladoras in great part because of their higher use of domestic inputs.[9]

Figure 3 shows that the interior maquiladoras have consistently used a higher proportion of domestic inputs than the border maquiladoras. While the logic of the assembly industry from the point of view of the foreign corporations is (or was originally) to take advantage of the cheap labor and provide all inputs from home, the long-term interests of the host country lie in creating a local supplier industry (see chapter 2 on Asian examples). Since the mid-seventies the Mexican government has exhorted both the maquiladoras to buy more local inputs and Mexican producers to produce for the maquiladoras (Sklair 1989: 197–199). As discussed in chapter 4, the foreign corporations may now be looking for more integrated clusters of suppliers in their overseas locations. Nevertheless, huge obstacles remain: Many sourcing decisions are still taken by home offices that are not aware of potential local suppliers; many Mexican producers cannot meet quality, quantity, or timeliness needs of the maquiladora plants.

With the increase in manufacturing and capital intensive technology the overall use of domestic inputs in the maquiladora industry has not improved. The national trend shown in Figure 3 is fairly steady at just under a paltry 1.5 percent of national inputs. In the interior, however, there has been a tendency for the use of domestic inputs to rise since the all-time low in 1985. In fact, the use of domestic inputs among maquiladoras in the interior doubled between 1985 and 1988. Breaking down these figures for the interior by sector shows contradictory trends (Table 12): The use of domestic inputs in electric and electronic equipment has risen since 1982, while in electric and electronics materials it has fallen. In transportation equipment it largely fell through 1985, after which there has been a gradual increase in the use of domestic inputs.

The only way to explain these trends and find the real story behind the growing linkages of the new maquiladoras in the interior is by direct survey. I posit that the new maquiladoras reflect in

Table 11 *Relative Growth of the Interior Maquiladoras, 1975–1990*

Year	No. of Plants			No. of Employees		
	Nation	Interior	% Interior	Nation	Interior	% Interior
1975	454	41	9.0	67,214	5,300	7.9
1976	448	47	10.5	74,496	7,200	9.7
1977	443	47	10.6	78,443	7,900	10.1
1978	457	39	8.5	90,704	8,600	9.5
1979	540	60	11.1	111,365	10,828	9.7
1980	620	69	11.1	119,546	12,970	10.8
1981	605	72	11.9	130,973	14,523	11.1
1982	585	71	12.1	127,048	13,821	10.9
1983	600	67	11.2	150,867	15,952	10.6
1984	672	77	11.5	199,684	22,775	11.4
1985	760	88	11.6	211,968	25,968	12.3
1986	890	120	13.5	249,833	37,542	15.0
1987	1,125	199	17.7	305,253	53,850	17.6
1988	1,396	256	18.3	369,489	70,626	19.1
1989	1,655	328	19.8	429,725	89,807	20.9
1990	1,938	n.a.	n.a.	460,293	n.a.	n.a.

Source: INEGI (1988, 1989, 1990, 1991).

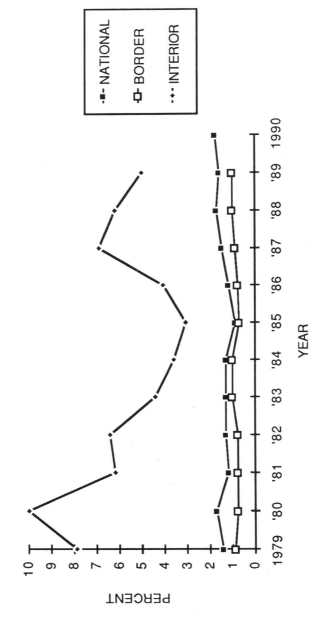

Figure 3. Use of Domestic Inputs, 1979–1990 (as percent of total inputs)

Source: INEGI (1988, 1989, 1990, 1991).

Table 12 *Use of Domestic Inputs by Selected Sectors in the Interior, 1980–1989 (percent of total inputs)*

	Transportation Equipment	Electric/ Electronic Equipment	Electric/ Electronic Materials	Total
1980	5.1	1.5	5.2	10.0
1981	3.3	1.5	3.6	6.2
1982	5.6	0.4	5.6	6.4
1983	6.2	0.2	6.2	4.4
1984	1.1	0.8	1.1	3.6
1985	0.8	1.4	0.8	3.1
1986	0.9	4.5	0.9	4.1
1987	2.4	9.8	1.0	6.9
1988	2.9	8.9	0.6	6.2
1989	2.4	7.3	1.1	5.0

Source: INEGI (1988, 1989, 1990: Table 10).

Note: Total includes the remaining sectors: clothing and textiles, footwear, furniture, chemicals, services, and the residual category, "other."

great part a strategic response to the changing global economy by both the multinationals and local producers. To get at the firms' strategies, their technology choices, and their sourcing patterns, the next three chapters go beyond the published data to draw on field survey results.

4. The Challenge of Flexible Manufacturing*

The maquiladora industry is at a historic crossroads with respect to its role in global corporate strategy. Will it continue to provide mainly a cost-saving respite for U.S. manufacturers faced with stiff international competition? Or will it find a role in the new corporate strategies of flexible production that permits a longer term competitive advantage in the global economy? The answers to these questions are crucial to both Mexican and U.S. economic policy. If the maquiladora industry is actually an incentive to complacency among U.S. producers (avoiding long-term productive restructuring in favor of short-term cost savings), then the maquiladoras may provide neither a sound competitive strategy for U.S. firms nor a sound development strategy for Mexico.

Some economic geographers (Womack 1987; Sanderson 1987; Schoenberger 1987) argue that foreign assembly plants such as maquiladoras will remain attractive primarily to those firms that are not pursuing the new strategies of flexible manufacturing. Flexible manufacturers, they posit, have less use for maquiladoras because their plants need to be close to R&D, just-in-time suppliers, and highly skilled labor. Maquiladora industry observers, on the other hand, point to a drastic change in the nature of maquiladoras since the peso devaluations in the early 1980s: Maquiladoras are no longer the purely labor intensive assembly plants of before. Many now manufacture and have adopted the management practices and even automated technology characteristic of forward-looking flexible producers, they say.

This chapter examines the rise of flexible production and its implications for maquiladoras. It discusses the conceptual supports

*An earlier version of this chapter was originally published in Fatemi (ed.), *The Maquiladora Industry* (Praeger Publishers, New York, an imprint of Greenwood Publishing Group, Inc., 1990), pp. 135–158. Copyright © 1990 by Khosrow Fatemi. Reprinted with permission.

and existing evidence for both sides of the argument as to whether the maquiladoras will play a role in the new flexible production strategies. The chapter then draws on an original survey to document empirically the growth of flexible production methods among the maquiladoras. It also documents the extent to which the maquiladoras have become more capital intensive manufacturers as opposed to labor intensive assembly plants. To shed light on the difference in local input use between the border and the interior, the chapter also examines how the new maquiladoras vary by location. The empirical analysis is based on a survey conducted on-site in late 1988 and early 1989 of seventy-one maquiladora plants located in three border cities and two interior cities. To provide a conceptual and historical context for the empirical analysis, the chapter begins with an explanation of the changing global competitive strategies—what many call the change from "Fordist" to "post-Fordist" strategies—and their implications for maquiladoras.[1]

The Rise of the Maquiladoras: Corporate Strategy during the Crisis of Mass Production

The period of mass industrialization and mass consumption was at its heyday in the United States in the two decades following World War II. The minute division of labor on the factory floor and large-scale standardized production allowed purchasing power for American factory workers to grow. From 1945 to 1965, U.S. corporations maintained global hegemony by following the mass production model.

In the developed countries, postwar mass production was the era of national consensus building between big capital and big labor. Collective bargaining, wage increases linked to productivity increases, a pervasive social security system, and a democratized educational system made the mass production model attractive to both capital and labor. Growing purchasing power for the majority of the population, along with increasing government consumption and investments, fed the economic growth cycle generously. The stable international and national economic climates (low inflation, monetary and financial stability) were also favorable to sustained national and personal income growth in the developed countries.[2]

By the end of the sixties, the first signs of disintegraton of the mass production era had become visible. In the developed countries near full-employment speeded up the growth of wage rates at the expense of profits and contributed to the satiation of demand in many markets. The U.S. balance of payments deficit left by the

Vietnam war shook the international monetary system, which was drastically reorganized. In August 1971 the convertibility of the dollar into gold was formally abandoned and national currency values were permitted to float on the international exchange markets. Thus international inflation was on the rise and the climate of economic stability essential to economic growth was eroding. The 1973 oil shock delivered the final blow to the golden age of capitalist mass production.

The maquiladora industry—and global assembly industry in general—grew during the late sixties and seventies as a corporate response to the emerging crisis in the mass production model. Declining profitability worldwide led corporations into an intensified competition to reduce costs and increase productivity by restructuring their operations. The restructuring was based on a combination of technological advances and geographical mobility that led to a new global location strategy. Technological advances in transportation, communications, and synthetics allowed location decisions to be disengaged from the traditional location determinants of proximity to markets or to raw materials. The new location strategy dissected the entire production process into discrete elements, each located so as to minimize costs. Thus, corporate administration and control functions, research and development, advanced manufacturing of prototypes, routine manufacturing, and labor intensive assembly could each be located optimally. (See the literature on the spatial implications of the product cycle, e.g., Vernon 1971, Rees 1979, Malecki 1983.)

In particular, the need to reduce labor costs (and increase labor stability) drove many companies to establish branch plants in greenfield locations (i.e., areas where the labor force was cheap and had little industrial or union experience) and to create parallel production facilities at two different locations, in order to play one off against the other in case of labor unrest. The resulting location strategy became dispersed, first on a regional scale (e.g., the south of the United States; see Hansen 1980) and then on a global scale (see the literature on the new international division of labor, e.g., Bluestone and Harrison 1982, Storper and Walker 1983, and Moulaert and Salinas 1983). Labor intensive assembly activities were the first to go offshore en masse, followed by higher value added manufacturing.

At first the global location strategy to reduce labor costs through the new international division of labor appeared to be the pinnacle of mass production rationality: mass production on a truly integrated global scale, represented by the expansive vision of the world car so vigorously (yet unsuccessfully) pursued by the Ford Motor Company (Cohen 1983). Yet in time the strategy became more a last ditch effort among leading firms to compete with newer—particularly Asian—firms that were unfettered by mass production practices.

By the early eighties it was clear that the mass production model had reached some of its productive and social limits which the global location strategy was not able to transcend. Productivity growth foundered. The minute division of labor that allowed workers to specialize in simple discrete tasks had turned into rigid job classifications that fostered worker alienation, lack of concern for quality, and disincentives to report problems or make suggestions. The far-flung corporate empires had created logistical problems with heavy costs. The huge investments in dedicated single purpose capital equipment hampered the ability to retool in response to changing market opportunities. The functional (and spatial) separation between R&D and manufacturing worked against the rapid incorporation of product innovations. The traditional mass production line necessitated large "just-in-case" inventories that tied up capital and required large factory floors.

By the early eighties the social limits of mass production were also visible in developed countries. Manufacturing workers began to be displaced, as corporations moved their jobs to lower labor cost sites. Increasing "locational capability" of plants, to use Storper and Walker's term (Storper and Walker 1983), led to high unemployment, or at least the threat of unemployment, and thus to a weakening of the labor unions and a decline in real wages (and demand). The decline in workers' earnings was exacerbated by selective technological innovations in the developed countries that deskilled substantial portions of the work process and further diminished the ranks of the well-paid workers/consumers (Noyelle, in Moulaert and Salinas 1983). As labor came to be seen more as a production cost to be minimized rather than a source of final demand, the social contract underlying the mass production model was fundamentally undermined.

In Mexico, as in much of Latin America, the decline of the mass production model was marked by the demise of import substitution and the rise of a neoliberal strategy of export promotion based on cheap labor. While an anomaly in the 1960s under import substitution, maquiladora investments grew as import substitution lost ground as a national development policy. By the 1980s the maquiladoras had become a priority sector in the new export-led development strategy.

For Mexico, the question now is whether or not the maquiladoras will survive the transition to flexible production that is altering corporate strategies for competing in the global economy.[3] The firms that maintain the old mass production strategies and compete mainly by spinning off production to cheap labor locations (or other unproductive measures such as mergers and acquisitions; see Reich 1983) may not ultimately survive in a global economy led by flexible producers.

The Emerging Corporate Strategy: Flexible Production

According to much of the new industrial literature, the firms with the greatest chance for long-term success will compete as flexible producers: small batch production, rather than mass production; product innovation rather than product standardization; responsiveness to rapidly changing market opportunities rather than dependence on mass markets; and quality competition over cost competition. In short, the new corporate strategy is characterized by flexibility, as developed by and used successfully in many Japanese corporations (Swyngedouw 1987).

Flexible or "post-Fordist" production differs from mass production in three ways: technology, the organization of work within factories, and the relations between firms. The technological change centers on the adoption of programmable automated machinery, which allows a variety of products or models to be produced without expensive retooling or costly downtime. Computer numeric controlled (CNC) tools, computer-aided design (CAD) and manufacturing (CAM), and robots can quickly incorporate changes. This "new generation of qualitatively distinct fixed capital" (Gertler 1988) permits firms to respond more quickly to changing market opportunities, to produce small batches with the low average costs previously achieved only by mass production, and to introduce rapid product and process innovations. This flexible technology can be much more cost-effective than traditional mass production with its dedicated single-purpose machinery. It permits a shortening of the product cycle, or the time between innovation and routine production. Finally, computerized scheduling and management of materials and information (through statistical process control [SPC], for example) permit reduced stocks and continuous quality control throughout the production process.

These flexible innovations begun in Japan and diffusing rapidly to North America and Europe involve not only the adoption of new technology but also a different method of deploying labor. The heart of mass production labor deployment is scientific management and Taylorism. Each worker is given a narrowly defined and simplified (i.e., deskilled) task, and a quality control department checks a sample of the final product for errors. Flexible manufacturing, on the other hand, involves rotating each worker through a variety of tasks, usually in a team context at a work station (rather than as individuals along an assembly line). Each team is responsible for a complete subproduct, including ongoing quality control and error prevention. Instead of punishing workers for halting production, management rewards them for stopping to investigate errors. Also under the flexible deployment of labor, workers are involved in quality circles, cooperative efforts involving labor and management to diagnose problems and propose solutions (see Swyngedouw 1987 on Japanese use of quality circles). The result of these flexible innovations is more efficient use of workers' time, knowledge, and experience, a greater sense of responsibility by the workers for their work, and sharply improved product quality (or drop in percent of rejects). Rather than antagonistic relations between management and labor, flexibility encourages cooperative relations between them.

Flexible manufacturing also implies different interfirm relations. Rather than vertical integration, common under mass production, the flexible strategy is to subcontract those activities for which the firm does not have a clear competitive advantage in producing themselves. Along with the rise of subcontracting, relations with suppliers become more crucial. Computer monitoring of the flow of materials allows parts inventories to be reduced to a minimum or to zero. This just-in-time inventory procedure contrasts sharply to the just-in-case approach associated with mass production. The just-in-time approach, however, requires much closer links with suppliers, who must be able to respond rapidly and with assured quality given the lack of buffer stocks. Thus flexible accumulation encourages fewer but larger and longer-term supplier contracts.[4] Producers offer an assured market in exchange for suppliers promising just-in-time supplies at highest possible quality levels.[5]

The electronics industry and the automobile industry were the first sectors in the United States to adopt flexible methods to a substantial degree.[6] Since U.S. electronics and automotive firms dominate the maquiladora industry (accounting for over 60 percent of maquiladora workers as of June 1988),[7] Mexico is quite vulnerable to changes in the organization and technology of production among these firms (Sanderson 1987: 128).[8]

The Maquiladora Industry at a Crossroads: The Spatial Implications of Flexible Production

Recent studies of location trends in the U.S. electronics industry (Sanderson 1987) and the U.S. automobile industry (Womack, 1987; Schoenberger 1987) point to a spatial reconcentration of flexible manufacturers back to the old (Fordist) industrial heartlands: While offshore assembly activities will continue to provide some jobs and revenues for developing countries for some time to come, their overall significance to the future economies of developed and developing countries is likely to be small. Instead of becoming the dominant production pattern, as some have predicted, coproduction activities may be marginalized and left to a few small producers who lack the capital and technical resources to automate. If U.S. firms continue to automate—as they surely must if they are to keep pace with the Japanese—then Mexico will suffer the direct loss of jobs and revenues associated with the products automated (Sanderson 1987: 140).

The argument that flexible production is incompatible with cheap labor locations rests on several legs. First, because flexible production shortens the product cycle (i.e., the length of time between product development and routine production), it will tend to pull R&D, advance manufacturing, and routine manufacturing spatially closer to one another than under the spatial division of labor associated with mass production. Rapid innovation and shorter product cycles obviate the rationale for reducing labor costs and labor skills as a product matures (Schoenberger 1987, 1988).

The second argument for spatial reconcentration is that flexible automation is labor saving, making labor cost less of a factor and enabling a return to higher wage regions. "Direct labor is becoming less important in the overall cost of many manufactured goods, and the increased use of computer-aided design and manufacturing (CAD/CAM) and robotics may erode the comparative advantage that low-wage regions currently hold for some important categories of manufacturing." Sanderson adds that Mexico's maquiladora industry is particularly vulnerable to this trend (Sanderson 1987: 127).

Third, the spatial reconcentration argument rests on the assumption that the technology and social relations of flexible production require a highly skilled and experienced labor force. In particular, team work, job rotation, and worker participation in problem diagnosis and quality control require more experienced and multiskilled (or "polyvalent," as Schoenberger 1987 and others refer to them) workers, who tend to be concentrated in the old industrial heartlands. "Given the increased demand for multi-skilled workers to fill those jobs which do remain, firms employing flexible technologies will naturally be reluctant to leave large metropolitan labor markets where such workers are most readily available" (Gertler 1988).

The changing relationship between producers and their suppliers or subcontractors under flexible accumulation is a fifth reason cited for spatial reconcentration (Sheard 1983; Estall 1985; Sayer 1985; Holmes 1986; Schoenberger 1987). Because producers using just-in-time systems do not maintain buffer stocks, small batches of parts and subassemblies must be available quickly in order not to halt the flow of production in the plant. Piore and Sabel (1984) add that the flexible producer (or "solar" firm, in their terms) requires proximity with suppliers because of the closer integration between them in terms of technology sharing, technical assistance, quality surveillance, and even ownership (e.g., joint ventures). Spatial proximity to suppliers is all the more important under flexible production because of the competitive strategies based on rapid product and process innovation, which causes rapid change in input needs. There is also a greater vulnerability to equipment breakdowns under flexible manufacturing (Schoenberger 1987) and therefore a greater need to remain close to specialized capital equipment repair services, including tool and die services. Malfunctions need to be repaired quickly to avoid downtime in the tightly integrated flexible production system.

The remaining argument in favor of spatial reconcentration is that producers of finished products will want to be closer to final markets to respond more quickly to changing market demand. Thus offshore locations would be disadvantageous in a corporate strategy aimed at rapid response to changing market opportunities.

Counter-arguments to the spatial reconcentration thesis attempt to show that there is no necessary incompatibility between a cheap labor location and flexible accumulation. One of the central counter-arguments questions the friction of distance. With telecommunications, computer linkages, and air travel, cannot information and expertise be communicated rapidly across borders (see Barrera 1988)? With respect to just-in-time suppliers, Mexico's proximity means that U.S. suppliers are only one to two days away by truck or rail and hours by air.[9] Moreover, large maquiladoras should be able to exercise their power over captive suppliers to get them to relocate nearby in order to establish local JIT networks.

The second counter-argument questions the assumption that a declining proportion of direct labor costs under flexible automation obviates the need to minimize labor costs. Even with flexible automation bringing labor costs down to 5 percent or less of total operating costs in some cases (Shaiken and Herzenberg 1988), the tight competition in today's global economy would still reward the flexible producer that can bring those costs down even further.

The third, and perhaps most important, counter-argument to the spatial reconcentration hypothesis is that an inexperienced labor force is not necessarily an obstacle to flexible production. In fact, it can be argued that experienced industrial workers are less flexible or adaptable because of their union history (see Shaiken et al. 1986). Traditional unions are often reluctant to permit fewer job classifications. They may not want to see the rigid demarcation between management and labor functions blurred through quality circles and other forms of labor participation. Greenfield sites may actually provide a labor force that is more adaptable to changes in the organization of work and the structure of decision making required by the new competitive strategies (Shaiken and Herzenberg 1988). Perhaps northern Mexico plays the role that Murray (1983) describes for the heralded Emilia-Romagna region of Italy as the locus of a well-developed putting-out system for large producers who want to break up their urban-based union-dominated factory complexes through a flexibly integrated but spatially decentralized system of subcontractors (or, in the case of the maquiladoras, subsidiaries).[10]

Another labor-related counter-argument to the spatial reconcentration hypothesis is that flexible automation and flexible work patterns do not require a large proportion of highly skilled workers. Job rotation and worker participation in problem diagnosis and continuous quality control may require a more flexible labor force but not necessarily a more skilled labor force. Similarly, the operation of flexibly automated machines may require nothing more than "simple push-button operations" and "simple product set-up and removal," as Robinson finds in the introduction of automated laser technology (1988: 223; see also Shaiken and Herzenberg 1988).

Finally, one may argue that factories may adopt flexible production practices gradually rather than all at once. Thus Third World sites could be somewhere on the flexibility learning curve, rather than not at all. Jaikumar (1986) shows that U.S. users of flexible manufacturing do not use it as thoroughly as do their Japanese counterparts.[11] Alternatively, Third World plants could selectively adopt aspects of flexible production in keeping with a cheap labor location; namely, the social organization of production rather than the expensive automated machinery.

Several studies provide empirical evidence that flexible manufacturing does occur in Mexico. Shaiken and Herzenberg (1988) document the use of flexible technology and shop floor practices in their in-depth case study of the Ford engine plant in Hermosillo. Robinson (1988) documents the use of flexible technology, shop floor practices, and interfirm relations (JIT) in two auto parts plants (one of which is a maquiladora) in northern Mexico. Carrillo V. (1989b) identifies a dozen auto plants in northern Mexico (several of which are maquiladoras) that use flexible technology, shop floor practices, and JIT. Boyce and Thakur (1988) report case studies of six manufacturing plants in Mexico, four of which have had some success in introducing participatory labor practices. From a survey of thirty-five electronics maquiladoras, Mertens and Palomares (1988, as cited in Carrillo V. 1989; see also Palomares and Mertens 1987) report a general tendency toward automation. Finally, maquiladora industry representatives along the border recount numerous anecdotes about state-of-the-art maquiladoras using robotics.[12] Nevertheless, these sectoral surveys, case studies, and anecdotal accounts do not permit a generalization about the extent of flexible production practices among maquiladoras; nor do they allow a careful distinction between maquiladoras of the interior and those of the border.

The rise of flexible production as a new corporate strategy raises doubts about the viability of labor-intensive assembly plants that were initiated in an area of mass production. The conceptual arguments about the heightened importance of spatially proximate transactional networks among manufacturers, their suppliers, and their subcontractors are strong. Yet the inference that these networks must be located in the industrial heartlands of the developed countries is weak. The conceptual door is left open to the possibility that these networks could occur in the Third World, thus allowing flexible production in low wage regions. The empirical evidence about flexible production in the maquiladora industry has been scanty. The next section reports new evidence from an original survey on the extent of flexible production in the maquiladora industry. To determine whether Mexico's maquiladora industry is playing a role in flexible manufacturing, an original survey was necessary that would go beyond the existing anecdotal accounts, sectoral studies, and government data. The survey needed to address to what extent the maquiladoras have adopted flexible production and what the implications are for local linkages, both in the interior and on the border.

Methodology

A total of 71 maquiladora plants were surveyed between November 1988 and March 1989. Follow-up interviews with 7 maquiladoras were conducted in late 1991 (Wilson 1992). Hour-long interviews using a common survey instrument were conducted on-site, usually with either the plant manager or the production manager.[13] These 71 plants represent 5.3 percent of the 1,333 maquiladora plants existing in Mexico in 1988 and 4.7 percent of the 350,286 maquiladora employees. Interior plants are disproportionately represented in the sample.[14] All 26 maquiladora plants in Guadalajara were interviewed and 15 out of 34 (44.1 percent) in Monterrey.[15] The interior sample frame (i.e., the total number of maquiladoras in Guadalajara and Monterrey) represents 25.3 percent of all interior maquiladora plants. Thirty border plants—10 each from Tijuana, Juárez, and Nuevo Laredo—were interviewed, representing 2.7 percent of all border plants and 3.0 percent, 4.1 percent, and 23.2 percent of the plants in each city, respectively. The border sample frame (i.e., the total number of maquiladoras in Tijuana, Juárez, and Nuevo Laredo) represents 57.1 percent of all border maquiladora plants.

To be considered a maquiladora, a plant had to be legally registered as a maquiladora and currently operating as a maquiladora.[16] The plants to be interviewed were selected to be representative of the sectoral and plant size mix for that city (except Guadalajara, where all were interviewed). A stratified random sample proved impossible in part because of incomplete knowledge about the universe (particularly, the number of workers in each plant in Monterrey) and in part because a number of plant managers along the border did not grant interviews.

As opposed to the in-depth case study approach (e.g., Shaiken and Herzenberg 1988) in which the investigator determines the shop floor methods and technologies being used, this broader survey used the manager's assessment of whether or not a particular method or technology was being used, the extent of its current use, and plans for future use.

Questions were asked about the extent to which the following characteristics of flexible production were present:

A. Production technology
    1. Computer-controlled production machinery[17]

B. Interfirm relations
1. Just-in-time (JIT) inventorying[18]
2. Subcontracting
C. Shop floor relations
1. Multiskilling/job rotation
2. Worker participation in
   a. problem diagnosis
   b. machine maintenance
   c. quality control
   d. Quality Circles
D. Management techniques
1. Statistical Process Control (SPC)
2. Continuous quality control (error prevention)
3. Use of temporary workers

The respondent had to assess the use of each of these practices in one of the following categories: (a) Yes, to a high degree; (b) Yes, to a moderate degree; (c) Yes, to a low degree; (d) No, but we are in the process of implementing it; (e) No, but we plan to introduce it in the next one to two years; or (f) No, and we do not intend to introduce it in the near future. The qualitative questions on JIT and the use of temporary workers were followed up with quantitative questions on the average length of incoming inventories on hand and the percent of temporary production workers. The manager was also asked to compare worker productivity (in terms of output per worker hour) with any parallel plants the parent firm owned in order to assess to what degree comparable technology was being employed in the Mexican plant. A distinction between manufacturing and assembly was made by asking the manager to assess whether the plant's function was primarily manufacturing or assembly, to what degree it manufactured, and whether there were plans to change in one direction or the other. Similarly, the manager was asked to characterize the plant as primarily labor-intensive or capital-intensive and to what degree. These qualitative questions were backed up with two quantitative questions on the amount of fixed capital invested per worker and the percent of total operating costs accounted for by labor.

The results allowed the plants to be classified into one of the following groups: flexible producers; mass production manufacturers; and traditional labor-intensive assembly plants. The main variable used to identify flexible producers was the technological one: the use of computer-controlled production machinery. Plants reporting a substantial use of computer-controlled production machinery (i.e., an answer of "a" or "b") were categorized as flexible producers. The main variable used to distinguish manufacturers from assembly plants was the manager's assessment of the relative degree of manufacturing versus assembly. Plants with a low degree of computer-controlled production machinery ("c" or below) and a high degree of manufacturing ("a" or "b") were classified as mass production manufacturers. Plants with a low degree of computer-controlled production machinery ("c" or below) and little or no manufacturing ("c" or below) were categorized as labor-intensive assembly plants. Categorizing the plants on the basis of these two variables produces the results shown in Table 13.

Flexible Producers

Eighteen percent of the plants (12 out of 68 responding) in the sample—or 21 percent on a weighted national level—fall into the category of flexible producers based on their use of computers in production.[19] Besides exhibiting a substantial ("a" or "b") use of computer-aided manufacturing, they also exhibit characteristic shop floor relations of flexible production (multiskilling and worker participation), management practices (continuous quality control and SPC), and interfirm relations (JIT) (see Table 14).[20] The one characteristic of flexible production that is definitely not present is subcontracting. The maquiladoras are at the bottom of the hierarchy of flexible subcontracting. The main sectors represented among the flexible maquiladoras are electronics and automotive: semiconductors, power supplies, transformers, electric cables, and wire harnesses for computers; electronic and plastic components for TVs and VCRs; metal, electronic, and electric components (mainly wire harnesses) along with solenoids and batteries for cars.

As to location, out of forty-one interior plants interviewed, six (or 15 percent) qualify as flexible producers, while six out of twenty-seven (or 22 percent) of the border plants qualify. Half of the flexible producers of the interior report a high ("a" or "b") use of JIT, as do half of those along the border; nevertheless, all the flexible producers of the interior are in the process of implementing ("d") or have implemented JIT to some degree. Thus not only is being in Mexico compatible with flexible technology and JIT, being in the interior of Mexico is compatible with flexible technology and JIT.

With respect to ownership, nine out of the twelve flexible producers are U.S.-owned (seven with 100 percent U.S. capital), two are Japanese, and one is Mexican.[21] Both of the Japanese plants were established in 1988, while all of the U.S. flexible producers in the

Table 13 *Maquiladora Plants by Type, 1988–1989*

	Total in Sample		Border		Guadalajara		Monterrey		Nation[e]
	N	%	N	%	N	%	N	%	%
Flexible producers[a]	12	18	6	22	3	12	3	20	21
Mass production manufacturers[b]	32	47	8	30	15	58	9	60	35
Labor-intensive assembly plants[c]	24	35	13	48	8	31	3	20	44
	68	100	27[d]	100	26	100	15	100	100

Source: Wilson survey of seventy-one maquiladora plants, 1988–1989.

[a]Those plants that have substantial (responding "a" or "b") use of computer-controlled production machinery. They also exhibit a high degree of other flexible production characteristics.

[b]Those plants with low or no use of computer-controlled machinery ("c"–"f"), but a substantial degree of manufacturing ("a" or "b").

[c]Those plants with low or no use of computer-controlled machinery ("c"–"f") and little or no manufacturing ("c"–"f").

[d]Only twenty-seven of the thirty border plants surveyed are used here. Two border plants surveyed were eliminated because they did not respond to the question on the degree of manufacturing (although neither used any computer-controlled machinery) and one was eliminated because it was a service provider (coupon counting) rather than a manufacturer or assembler.

[e]Weighted by regional plant population sizes to reflect importance of border.

Table 14 Characteristics of Maquiladora Plants by Type

	Flexible Producers $N = 12^a$	Mass prodn. Mfrs. $N = 32^a$	Labor-intensive Assembly $N = 24^a$	Total[i] $N = 68^a$
Production technology				
Computer-controlled machinery[b]	100%	0%	0%	18% ± 9
Manufacturing-oriented[b]	33%	100%	0%	53% ± 12
Capital intensive[b]	33%	28%	17%	25% ± 10
Labor costs as percentage of total operating costs[c]	53%	34%	56%	46% ± 8
Interfirm relations				
JIT[b]	42%[h]	9%	25%	19% ± 9
Subcontracting[b]	0%	13%	3%	6% ± 6
Shop floor practices				
Multiskilling[b,i]	50%	39%	21%	34% ± 12
Worker participation[b]	75%	29%	46%	42% ± 12
Management practices				
Continuous quality control[b]	92%	81%	88%	85% ± 8
SPC[d]	75%	28%	58%	53% ± 12

Labor force characteristics			
Percent female	66%	51%	63%	59% ± 7
Percent temporaries	11%	21%	13%	17% ± 7
On-the-job training[e]	4.0 wks	7.1 wks	1.6 wks	5.1 ± 1.7
Other				
Ownership: Percent U.S.[f]	75%	53%	67%	62% ± 12
Percent Mexican[g]	8%	31%	25%	25% ± 10
Size (no. line workers)	556	143	222	270 ± 94
Year established (av.)	1981	1984	1983	1983 ± 1
Percent since 1982	50%	75%	75%	71% ± 11
Percent since 1986	33%	56%	46%	46% ± 12

Source: Wilson survey, 1988–1989.

[a]Except where indicated.

[b]Percent with substantial use (i.e., responding "a" or "b").

[c]n = 5, 20, and 13, respectively.

[d]Percent with some use (i.e., responding "a," "b," or "c").

[e]n = 3, 9, and 4, respectively.

[f]Percent of plants with at least 40 percent U.S. capital.

[g]Percent of plants with at least 60 percent Mexican capital.

[h]Another 33 percent said they were currently in the process of implementing JIT (compared to 16 percent of the manufacturers and 0 percent of the labor intensive assemblers).

[i]N = 10, 28, and 24, respectively.

[j]Approximate 95 percent confidence limits shown.

sample are older.[22] The bulk of the U.S. flexible producers—especially in the interior—are the older large maquiladoras started in the late sixties and seventies that have recently converted to flexible technology and methods. Examples include the Unisys (formerly Burroughs) plant that started in Guadalajara in 1968, had 790 production workers in 1988, and closed in 1991; the Motorola plant that started in Guadalajara in 1969 and grew to 2,440 production workers by 1988; and the Delco (General Motors) plant started in Juárez in 1973, with 1,346 production workers in 1988.

Automated production processes controlled by computer include plastic injection molding for making television components and cassette tape holders, plastic component milling and buffing for spray bottles, wiring of computer keyboards, laser printing of symbols on keyboard components, soldering and washing of electric wires, autosplicing to insert electric terminals in surge supressors, and chip insertion on printed circuit boards, and cutting, milling, drilling, welding, and painting of metal. Computers are used even more extensively in nonproductive shop floor activities: quality control and statistical process control.

None of the plants, however, is fully automated. Few do R&D other than to adapt designs and processes from the parent company to their own shop floor configurations. Several of the flexible producers in the sample maintain the traditional labor intensive assembly lines along with automated lines in order to respond to market opportunities in either venue. Many have traditional assembly lines as their major activity but have automated a few of the processes. Only a third of the flexible producers in the sample are manufacturing-oriented. Most do predominantly assembly with some manufacturing ("c"). The degree of capital intensity varies widely ("a" to "f"), although a third rate themselves as substantially capital intensive ("a" or "b"). The percent of total costs due to labor also varies widely, from 12 percent to 70 percent, with an average of 53 percent (based on five firms responding). While the flexible maquiladora plants represent a technological advancement over their more traditional counterparts, they do not represent the full-fledged flexible automation characteristic of many flexible producers in developed countries.

Neither have these flexible producers developed a domestic supplier network. Of all three types of maquiladoras, the flexible producers use the smallest proportion of domestic inputs, regardless of location. They continue to source almost totally from U.S. suppliers, maintaining what the managers consider JIT inventories with long-distance relationships. Table 15 shows that the flexible pro-

Table 15. A. Average Percent of Local Inputs Used in Maquiladoras by Type of Plant and Location, 1988–1989

Type of Plant	Sample	Border	Guadalajara	Monterrey	Nation[b]
Flexible Producers[a]	1.7	0.0	6.0	0.7	0.5
Mass Production Manufacturers	14.5	2.6	10.5	31.9	6.2
Labor Intensive Assembly	3.1	0.0	9.2	3.3	1.1
Average	8.1	0.7	9.6	19.9	3.4

B. Average Percent of National Inputs Used in Maquiladoras by Type of Plant and Location, 1988–1989

Type of Plant	Sample	Border	Guadalajara	Monterrey	Nation
Flexible producers	2.6	0.0	9.7	0.7	0.8
Mass production manufacturers	31.0	17.1	31.0	43.3	20.9
Labor Intensive Assembly	7.0	3.6	13.3	6.7	4.7
Average	17.4	6.3	23.9	27.5	9.9

Source: Wilson survey, 1988–1989.

[a]Flexible producer; measured as those plants that have substantial use of computer-controlled production machinery. They also exhibit a high degree of other flexible production characteristics.

Mass production manufacturer; measured as those plants with low or no use of computer-controlled machinery, but a substantial degree of manufacturing.

Labor-intensive assembly plant; measured as those plants with low or no use of computer-controlled machinery and little or no manufacturing.

[b]Weighted average to reflect predominance of border region (82 percent of national total).

ducers surveyed along the border source none of their productive inputs in Mexico; even those in the industrial city of Monterrey behave as enclaves, sourcing less than 1 percent of their productive inputs domestically. The flexible producers of Guadalajara evidence the highest degree of national inputs compared to the other locations, making Guadalajara a useful case study to see what gives rise to the higher linkages among flexible producers there. Chapter 5 treats the Guadalajara case in detail.

The flexible maquiladora plants use as high a proportion of female workers as do the traditional assembly plants (Table 15). In their survey of thirty-five electronics maquiladoras, Palomares and Mertens (1987) also found that female workers constituted well over half the manual workers and machine operators in both those without automation (68 percent), and those having automation (66 percent).[23]

Similarly, the occupational structure in maquiladoras that use programmable machinery varies only slightly from those that do not.[24] Palomares and Mertens (1987) found in their survey of thirty-five electronics maquiladoras that in those which did not have programmable equipment, manual workers and machine operators made up 85 percent of the direct labor force, while in those that did use programmable machinery, the percentage was 81 percent (compared to a much lower 41 percent in the United States). Technicians increased from 8 to 12 percent and engineers from 2 to 5 percent in the electronics maquiladoras with programmable machinery compared to those without. These findings are reinforced by Carrillo V.'s (1989b) survey of auto plants in Mexico which found that among Ford's maquiladoras (which use programmable machinery) there were only twelve skilled workers for every one hundred unskilled (Carrillo V. 1989b: 12). There is some evidence that the wage structure in the flexible firms parallels the occupational structure: Carrillo V. (1989b) reports that almost all the line workers and machine operators that he interviewed in the auto maquiladoras—automated and nonautomated—received minimum wage (plus social security benefits, company benefits such as transportation and lunches, and company bonuses, such as punctuality and attendance rewards).[25]

The findings support the contention that flexible production and a low wage location are not incompatible, that some of Mexico's maquiladora industry is adopting flexible production methods to a substantial degree—in technology, shop floor relations, management practices, and interfirm relations. Furthermore, these practices are not confined to the border. Distance—to suppliers, markets, R&D, and skilled labor—does not seem to be an insurmountable obstacle to flexible production. Nevertheless, the flexible producers have adapted to their cheap labor context with low wages, short job ladders, a largely female labor force, little or no R&D, no fully integrated flexible manufacturing, and even a higher degree of imported inputs than among the other maquiladoras. The result is a caricature of the flexible production being experienced in the advanced countries.

Labor Intensive Assembly Plants

On a national level the single largest category of maquiladoras is still the labor intensive assembly plant, representing 44 percent of the total. These maquiladoras show little or no use of computers in production and little or no manufacturing. They use a small amount of Mexican inputs, although more than the flexible producers use (see Table 15). They use predominantly female labor (63 percent) in jobs that require very little training. These more traditional maquiladoras are most heavily represented along the border, typifying almost half the border sample, and are found principally in electronics and electric equipment. The highest degree of Mexican ownership is also evident in this group but reflects primarily interior maquiladoras in shoes and furniture. The plants in this group are not aging leftovers of a bygone era either, as 75 percent of them were established after 1982 and nearly half of them since 1986.

While labor intensive assembly is still a thriving growth sector of the maquiladora industry, there are some changes: A third of them are using SPC to a substantial degree and a fourth of them are using JIT to a substantial degree (not all the same firms either). In other words, some of these labor intensive assembly plants are adopting some of the practices of flexible production without making the heavy investments in automated technology. It may be that redeployable labor, as opposed to reprogrammable machines, provides sufficient flexibility and quality for the markets these plants are currently producing for.[26]

Mass Production Manufacturers

The most rapidly growing segment[27] of the maquiladora industry is that of the mass production manufacturers; that is, the maquiladoras that do a substantial degree of manufacturing ("a" or "b"), but without the flexible technology. The rapid growth of the manufacturing plants reflects the changing role of Mexico in the international division of labor, as mass production manufacturers spin off not only labor intensive assembly operations to Third World locations but also manufacturing for reexport. These plants manufacture chemicals, plastic goods, glass, ceramic products, food, basic metals, electric and nonelectric equipment, air conditioners, electric motors, sports equipment, textiles, jewelry, furniture, shoes, auto parts, and electronic equipment.

The manufacturers are much more prevalent in the interior than along the border. Fifteen (or 58 percent) of the twenty-six maquiladora plants in Guadalajara fall into the category of manufacturers, as do nine (or 60 percent) of the fifteen firms in Monterrey, and eight (30 percent) of the twenty-seven border plants. As shown in Table 14, the manufacturers evidence a much higher degree of Mexican ownership than do the flexible producers: 31 percent, compared to 17 percent. But this difference does not hold among the newer manufacturers: Only 11 percent (from n = 18) of the manufacturing plants that have been established since 1986 are of Mexican ownership. The manufacturers show the highest use of male production workers, compared to both the flexible producers and the labor intensive assembly plants, and the longest average on-the-job training periods. The manufacturers show very little use of JIT and relatively little use of SPC and worker participation. They are smaller in size than the average maquiladora, younger, and more rapidly proliferating: Three-fourths of them have been established since 1982 and over half of them (56 percent) since 1986.

It is the manufacturers that account for the higher degree of domestic content among the maquiladoras of the interior (Table 15). For the entire industry, the average percent of national inputs used by the manufacturers is over four times higher than that for labor intensive assembly plants and over twenty-five times higher than that for flexible producers. The relationship is more pronounced for Monterrey: Manufacturers use over six times the percent of national inputs that labor intensive assembly plants use and over sixty times that of the flexible producers. The relationship for Guadalajara is consistent but less pronounced: The manufacturers use over twice the proportion of domestic inputs as do the labor intensive assembly plants and three times that of the flexible producers. Roughly similar findings hold for the use of local inputs (i.e., inputs manufactured in the local metropolitan area) as well (Table 15).

Conclusions

The maquiladora industry is finding a role in the new competitive strategy of flexible production. Computer-controlled machinery is being used to mold plastic components, wire computer keyboards, insert chips on printed cirucit boards, and weld and paint metal. About 20 percent of the maquiladora plants surveyed can be considered flexible producers in that they employ a substantial degree of computer-controlled machinery. They also exhibit many of the other characteristics of flexible production, for example, just-in-time inventory methods; multiskilling of production workers and job rotation; worker participation in problem diagnosis, machine maintenance, and quality control; continuous quality control and error prevention; and statistical process control. Follow-up interviews in late 1991 with seven maquiladoras show that the plants are continuing to adopt flexible production methods (Wilson 1992).

The presence of these flexible producers is not limited to the border. Twelve percent of Guadalajara's maquiladoras fall into the category, as do 20 percent of those sampled in Monterrey. The increased distance to U.S. suppliers does not prevent any of them from using JIT to at least a low degree. In fact, the same proportion of flexible maquiladoras use it to a substantial degree in both the border and the interior.

In addition to the flexible producers, there is a sizeable proportion of plants—mainly labor intensive assembly plants—that are adopting some of the soft forms of flexible production, such as shop floor relations, management practices, and JIT. In other words, they are avoiding the huge outlays for computer-controlled machinery but adopting some of the practices more consistent with a low cost labor location.

Nevertheless, the rise of flexible producers among Mexico's maquiladoras has created so far only a caricature of flexible production. Even those plants reporting a substantial use of programmable machinery have limited its use so as not to obviate the labor intensive nature of the maquiladora operation or even its reliance on a feminine work force. The rise of flexible producers is not accompanied by an autonomous R&D capability or by economic autonomy. Far from being a Third Italy of small autonomous producers able to capitalize on the economies of flexible automation at a small scale, the flexible maquiladoras are almost all divisions or subsidiaries of large U.S. (or Japanese) corporations. Neither is the increased involvement and responsibility of the workers in the flexible production plants accompanied by a noticeable improvement in the social contract in terms of wages, job ladders, autonomy on the job, or bargaining power.[28] Finally, the entry of flexible production into the maquiladora industry indicates even less domestic sourcing, both on the border and in the interior.

The rise of flexible producers in the maquiladora industry is not the whole story of the new maquiladoras, however. Only a minority of maquiladora plants are playing a role in U.S. corporate strategies of flexible production. U.S. producers are using the maquiladora industry primarily for mass production manufacturing operations as well as more traditional labor intensive assembly in order to reduce costs without fundamentally restructuring operations. The most rapidly growing segments of the maquiladora industry are the manufacturers—especially in the interior—and the labor intensive assembly plants—especially along the border.

The phenomenal rise of the manufacturers in the maquiladora industry may be more beneficial to Mexico in the long run, however, than the growth of either the traditional labor intensive assembly plants or the flexible maquiladoras. The manufacturing plants evidence a greater degree of national inputs, greater use of male workers, and more on-the-job training. But if the global economy is in a transition to flexible production, the long run for mass production manufacturing may be very limited. If maquiladoras continue to be a priority sector in its national development strategy, Mexico must figure out how to get the most out of an export-oriented mass production strategy in the short run or how to avoid a caricature of flexible production in the long run.

5. Maquiladoras and Local Linkages: Transaction Networks in Guadalajara

For Mexico's assembly industry to be more than a source of foreign exchange and low-paying jobs, the maquiladora plants must create linkages with the local economy. These linkages occur through the network of transactions that the plant creates with local firms; for example, the purchase of locally manufactured inputs and local services, subcontracting to local firms, the sale of products as inputs to local manufacturers, and the creation of spin-off firms. Each transaction serves as a possible conduit for technology transfer and an impetus to more diversified job opportunities. This chapter examines the transaction network of the maquiladora industry in the large interior city of Guadalajara to see where the local linkages are strong and where they are tenuous. This transactional analysis is based on in-plant surveys of all twenty-six of Guadalajara's maquiladoras. The case of Guadalajara is contrasted with Monterrey and the northern border to show that public sector efforts to encourage the local transaction network of the maquiladora industry would have to be tailored to the particular city or region.

In Guadalajara there are two large clusters of maquiladoras, each with its own pattern of local networks. One is the sector of mostly small, home-grown, craft-based maquiladoras in apparel, footwear, furniture, jewelry, and toys. These maquiladoras represent the tip of a long-standing craft sector in Guadalajara. The other large cluster of maquiladoras is the electronics sector: foreign subsidiaries, many quite large, producing electronics components and subassemblies. The electronics maquiladoras form a part of Guadalajara's much larger electronics industry, which includes foreign plants that are not maquiladoras but do export, joint ventures between foreign and Mexican capital, and locally owned start-ups. In addition to the crafts cluster and the electronics cluster, there is a small cluster of auto part maquiladoras, primarily U.S. branch plants, attracted in the late 1970s and early 1980s to Guadalajara by the local metalworking industry.

Conceptual Framework

Mexico has opted for an export-led development strategy. One of the pitfalls of such a strategy is the reliance on foreign capital, technology, raw materials, and markets. The result can be an isolated enclave of export-oriented manufacturing that does not create a broad-based internal industrialization. This risk is particularly high with foreign assembly industry, such as Mexico's maquiladora industry. By their very nature foreign assembly plants tend to be industrial enclaves. They are rewarded with tax exonerations for bringing in raw materials and machinery from abroad and exporting the output. And in fact the record shows that after twenty-five years the maquiladoras in general source less than 2 percent of their raw materials domestically (INEGI).[1] Yet the government of Mexico continues to vigorously promote the maquiladora industry as part of its overall export-led industrialization strategy, encouraging plants to locate in the interior, where they have shown a greater tendency to source domestically.

The changing global economy points to a possible new opportunity for creating greater local linkages from the maquiladora industry: the rise of flexible production (Swyngedouw 1987; Gertler 1988; Schoenberger 1987). As a corporate strategy aimed at meeting Japanese competition, flexible production emphasizes quality competition over cost competition and adaptability to changing market opportunities over production for a standardized mass market. Economies of scope overshadow economies of scale as flexibility becomes the hallmark of the competitive edge. Vertical disintegration replaces vertical integration as large producers unburden themselves of all but their most productive or technologically sensitive endeavors in the pursuit of flexibility. What replaces the vertically integrated global complexes of mass production is a series of tightly integrated multifirm networks of buyers, suppliers, and subcontractors.

These networks have a spatial dimension to them. The need for just-in-time deliveries, the careful sharing of technology, and the supervising of quality control between firms create the need for geographical clustering of these networks that telecommunications cannot totally obviate. While many observers have predicted that the rise of flexible production will bring the far-flung corporate empires back home (e.g., Sanderson 1987; Schoenberger 1987), others admit the possibility of clustering in Third World locations (e.g., Scott 1989). The Mexican government needs to foster local networking among these clusters. The electronics cluster in Guadalajara, which already has been dubbed Mexico's Silicon Valley by some of the international business press, holds particular potential.

The rise of flexible production also creates a new opportunity for small-scale producers to enter the international market without an inherent disadvantage from the lack of economies of scale. In fact, the economic development literature has formalized a craft paradigm modelled after the successful entry of North Central Italy's locally owned craft shops, particularly in textiles and clothing, into the international market (Piore and Sabel 1984; Scott 1989; Hatch 1987). The basis of their success has been networking and cooperation among the local small firms. The Mexican government should seek ways to promote local networking for export among Guadalajara's craft industries.

Economic Development in Guadalajara

Until the 1930s, Guadalajara was a commercial center serving the large landowners in the surrounding agricultural region. Trade was dominated by a few powerful merchants. Beginning in the 1930s the merchants diversified into the production of consumer articles for the regional market, primarily by subcontracting to small workshops of craft producers using temporary, family, and home workers, largely female. By the mid-1960s other urban centers in the region had grown up and begun to take over some of the region-serving commercial functions of Guadalajara. The Guadalajaran oligarchy entered manufacturing on a larger scale, often employing craft workers in formal factories such as that of the nationally known shoe manufacturer, Canadá (Escobar 1988: 7–8). At the same time Mexican capital from outside the region—both domestic and foreign—began to set up factories in Guadalajara. Outside manufacturers were attracted in part by the growing regional market and industrial infrastructure but also by the cooperative, trained labor force.

The first U.S.-owned maquiladoras arrived in Guadalajara in the late 1960s. The presence of a female industrial labor force stemming from the craft industries was particularly attractive to them (Gabayet 1983). Burroughs (later Unisys), arriving in 1968, employed 80 percent (about 640) women line workers before it closed in 1991. Motorola, arriving in 1969, employs 70 percent (about 1,750) women line workers. General Instrument (now owned by C. P. Clare) and

TRW (since bought out by Shizuki), arriving in 1973–74, employ 80 to 90 percent women line workers (450 to 500 each).

Foreign auto part maquiladoras started showing up in the late 1970s. They use a predominantly male labor force. Attracted by the existing metal mechanics industry and its labor force, Borg Warner opened up two auto parts plants, one in 1978 and one in 1980. Another U.S. auto plant producer, Reliance Electric, and a Spanish auto parts manufacturer both established maquiladoras in 1981.

Most of the maquiladoras in Guadalajara have been established since the crisis of 1982, largely in crafts (eight plants) and electronics (three), with one each in home appliances, auto parts, plastics, and chemicals. The 1980s also witnessed the growth of nonmaquiladora manufacturing plants, especially in electronics (see below). The state of Jalisco, reflecting Guadalajara's growth, more than doubled its share in total foreign investment in Mexico from 1.7 percent in 1982 to 3.8 percent in 1987 (see DEPRODE for 1988). The maquiladora growth rate for Jalisco, which also reflects the Guadalajara metropolitan area, exceeded both that of the border and the interior for these years in terms of number of plants, but not in terms of number of employees (see Appendix 1).

Methodology

To analyze the transaction network of Guadalajara's maquiladoras requires detailed plant-level information on sourcing patterns, marketing, and new firm spin-offs: where the inputs—both goods and services—come from; where the outputs are sold; and what additional companies have been created by the firm itself or by employees of the firm. The information must be geographically specific to distinguish which purchases, sales, and spin-offs are local, which domestic, and which foreign. The geographic information on goods purchased must refer to the point of manufacture of the goods—not the point of distribution. While the Mexican government (INEGI) records the amount of domestic inputs used by each maquiladora, the published data allow only a broad sectoral or geographic analysis of the plants by average percent of national inputs used, and only for goods—not services. The Mexican government does not gather data on inputs manufactured in the local metropolitan area. Heretofore, information on local inputs purchased by maquiladoras has been purely anecdotal.

For this transactional analysis all twenty-six maquiladora plants in Guadalajara were interviewed, providing 100 percent coverage (two responses, both from small plants, were thrown out because of inconsistent answers). Plant managers were asked to specify the degree and nature of four kinds of local linkages: (1) local productive inputs purchased (i.e., raw materials used in the production process that are manufactured in the local metropolitan area); (2) local productive services purchased (specific questions were asked about tool and die, metal stamping, and plastic molding);[2] (3) sales made locally; and (4) local spin-off companies started. Follow-up questions were asked about the names of local manufacturers, service providers, and spin-off firms in order to subsequently survey a selection of local suppliers and spin-offs about their sourcing patterns. Questions were also asked about the degree and nature of nonlocal domestic inputs (i.e., from elsewhere in Mexico). Finally, respondents were asked to rank location factors to determine in which cases access to local goods and services was considered important.

Crafts Network

"Maquilization" of Crafts

Most craft industries responded to the fall of the internal market in 1982 in one of two ways (Escobar 1988: 10): Some began to deformalize the work process again by increasing home work and temporary work, not paying taxes, and scaling back to family-sized operations. The lack of operating capital made others decide to return to subcontracting for larger companies in Guadalajara. However, there was another strategy followed that has not been noted in the literature: the "maquilization" of the crafts industries. Faced with a falling internal market and capital shortages, a number of craft manufacturers sought maquiladora status in order to produce for the export market and find a U.S. client who would provide most of the raw materials. Some did not like either the red tape or the vagaries of the foreign client's demands and subsequently stopped using their special legal status. In visiting craft manufacturers registered as maquiladoras we found several who were no longer operating as such. Ten craft producers, however, were actively operating as registered maquiladoras at the time of the survey in 1988–89.

The relatively high use of local inputs among Guadalajara's maquiladoras is accounted for largely by the crafts producers (see Table 16). An average of 16 percent of the inputs used by the ten crafts producers are made in the Guadalajara metropolitan area. Most of these craft-producing maquiladoras are small, locally owned companies in footwear, furniture, clothing, jewelry, and toys. Unlike maquiladoras in the same sectors along the border, the ones in Guadalajara have emerged from a strong local tradition of craft manufacturing for the domestic market. In fact, seven of the ten craft manufacturers operating as maquiladoras in Guadalajara sell also on the domestic market, four of them a minor portion of their output and three of them the majority of their output. The latter use maquiladora status primarily as excess capacity warrants. An eighth plant—one of the clothing manufacturers—existed as a factory for the domestic market before restructuring recently as a maquiladora exporting all of its output. Almost all have started operations as maquiladoras since the 1982 crisis, and most since 1987.

Technology

Unlike the craft maquiladoras along the border, most of these maquiladoras do not offer just contract labor services to simply assemble inputs brought in by a North American client firm. The plant managers in fully 70 percent of them characterized their maquiladora production process as being largely manufacturing as opposed to assembly.[3] Many of the craft-based firms in Guadalajara add value to the product by cutting, forming, molding, dying, and painting, in addition to the more traditional labor intensive assembly of stitching and joining. On the other hand, none of them go beyond the mass production model to adopt the techniques of flexible manufacturing. Almost all of them reported no use of computer-controlled machinery or just-in-time inventorying or had any plans to introduce them in the future (see Appendix 2).

Local Inputs

Guadalajara's craft-based maquiladoras use more local inputs on average than do any other cluster (Table 16). The toy firm, which manufactures mylar (metallic) balloons, uses locally made photopolymer engravings for each design and adds locally manufactured plastic sticks and connectors. Nevertheless, it imports most of its major raw material, nylon. The footwear producers get their main raw materials largely from their U.S. clients both for leather and synthetic shoes. However, they do buy locally manufactured tacks, nails, glue, thread, and dyes. The furniture manufacturers, whose raw materials come largely from the United States, also buy locally manufactured rivets, tacks, solder, screws, wood, glues, nails, and staples. Of the two apparel plants, one buys no local inputs and the

Table 16 *Characteristics of Guadalajara's Maquiladoras by Sector, 1988–1989*

Sector	No. of Plants	Average % Local Inputs	Average % Natl. Inputs	% Foreign-owned	Year Established (average)	Average No. of Workers	Average % Female
Crafts	10	16	23	0	1984	45	65
Toys	1	40	70	0	1984	70	60
Furniture	2	25	43	0	1987	28	43
Footwear	4	10	15	0	1983	65	54
Textiles and clothing	2	8	8	0	1983	21	100
Jewelry	1	10	10	0	1985	28	86
Electronics	6	2	6	100	1978	749	72
Auto Parts	5	4	37	100	1982	59	38
Other	3	10	45	100	1987	90	85
Appliances	1	30	35	100	1988	24	95
Plastics	1	0	96	100	1985	97	80
Chemicals	1	0	0	100	1987	150	80

Source: Wilson survey, 1988–1989.

other buys thread and glues from local manufacturers. The manufacturer of fine jewelry buys locally produced industrial gases.

While this use of local inputs is unusually high for maquiladoras, it is not for domestic industry. According to plant managers (often owners) who produce for the internal market in addition to their maquiladora operations, their export production uses fewer local inputs than does their domestic-oriented production. The difference is due primarily to the fact that their U.S. clients provide most of the inputs.

National Inputs

Several of the craft-based maquiladoras also use significant raw materials from elsewhere in Mexico (see national inputs in Table 16, which are a sum of local and nonlocal domestic inputs). The balloon manufacturer gets a part of its major input, nylon, and some of its dyes from both Mexico City and Monterrey. One of the furniture makers, which makes waterbeds, gets some of its wood, paint, and varnish from elsewhere in Mexico. However, its principal input, plastic cloth, comes from the United States. Other furniture makers buy metal stampings from the state of México and Monterrey. The shoe manufacturers buy some of their chemicals and plastics (for synthetic shoes) from Mexico City and Puebla. A small portion of leather comes from León. The jewelry maker gets a small portion of its gold from Mexico City.

Other Transactions

While the craft maquiladoras use a comparatively high amount of local inputs compared to the other maquiladoras, they use few local manufacturing services and have created no spin-offs that we could identify. In terms of local manufacturing services, only two of the ten use local tool and die and two use local plastic molding. None uses local metal stamping. Most get their plastic molding from their principal U.S. client and have their metal stamping done in either Mexico City or the United States.

Unlike the domestic craft producers in Guadalajara, which subcontract much of their work and employ a high proportion of temporary workers (Escobar 1988), only one footwear firm among the maquiladora craft factories does a large amount of subcontracting and none rely on temporary employees. While the maquiladoras provide jobs that are more protected and regulated than in most of the smaller craft plants, they do not experience the fluid interaction among firms that the domestic craft producers are known for.

Electronics Network

Maquiladoras

The six electronics maquiladoras use a very small percentage of local inputs, varying from o to 6 percent. Neither do they use substantial Mexican inputs from elsewhere in the country. Nevertheless, a substantial proportion of them do use local productive services and have created some important spin-offs. Moreover, the sheer size of some of them means that while the percentage of local inputs is small the volume is important.

The six electronics maquiladoras are all fully owned subsidiaries of foreign firms, five U.S. and one Japanese. Unlike the crafts maquiladoras, these plants are an outgrowth of foreign industry, having been established from the beginning as complete maquiladoras exporting nearly all their outputs. They include the three oldest maquiladoras of Guadalajara: Unisys (formerly Burroughs), General Instrument (now C. P. Clare), and Motorola. These large plants were all established in the late sixties and early seventies and employed between 500 and 2,500 line workers each in 1988. The other three (Tulon [Easterline], Digital Power, and Shizuki) were established since 1985.[4] The newer plants are smaller, ranging from under 50 production workers up to 650 in the case of Shizuki. The older plants produce electric cable assemblies and wiring harnesses for computers, power supplies, semiconductors, electronic voltage surge supressors, and relays. The newer plants make power supplies, circuit board drills, and capacitors.

Technology.   Only three maquiladora plants in Guadalajara make substantial use of computer-controlled production machines, a key element of flexible technology. Two of them are electronics firms, the two largest and oldest electronics maquiladoras in Guadalajara—Unisys and Motorola. Unlike General Instrument, Unisys and Motorola significantly updated their technology and shop floor methods in the 1980s to incorporate some flexible production capabilities. While these two do use more local productive inputs than the other electronics maquiladoras (4 percent on average compared to .5 percent for the other electronics maquiladoras), this may reflect the time they have had to develop some local suppliers rather than some inherent tendency of the technology. Certainly, the use

of just-in-time inventorying is not associated with greater local inputs (see Appendix 3). While all but one of the six electronics maquiladoras use JIT or are in the process of implementing it, they
reported that they do so with inputs coming from the United States.

Local and National Inputs.   Unisys, which made electronic cables, harnesses, and power supplies for Unisys equipment before it
closed in 1991, got most of its raw materials from Unisys in Dallas.
It bought only metal chassis made in Guadalajara and terminals
and connectors made in Mexico City. The Motorola Semiconductor
plant, which manufactures wafers, brings in all the chip parts from
the United States and Europe. Some chemicals are purchased in
Monterrey. The only local productive input is industrial gases from
the Union Carbide plant in Guadalajara. The plant also purchases
local packing material. General Instrument has been unable to find
good local suppliers but is talking to IBM about its local suppliers
such as U.S.-owned ADTEC for double-sided high density printed
circuit boards and U.S.-owned Cherokee for power supplies. Taking
all the electronics maquiladoras together, the main local productive
inputs are industrial gases, metal chassis, varnish, wire, screws, and
tools. Nonproductive local materials include packaging materials
such as cartons, dry ice, and styrofoam and rubber boots and uni-
forms for workers.

As to national inputs from elsewhere in Mexico, a few of the
electronics maquiladoras get gases and chemicals from Monterrey
(in fact, Motorola helped to set up some of these suppliers); machine parts, lubricants, screws, tools, and coolants from Mexico City;
and solvents, solder, and casting agents from both Mexico City and
San Luis Potosí. The Unisys general manager said that the plant
bought cables and connectors assembled in Mexico City but was
setting up suppliers in San Luis Potosí and San Juan del Río to manufacture cables and connectors using 50 percent domestic content.

Spin-offs.   The older electronics maquiladoras—Unisys, Motorola,
and General Instrument—have generated three local spin-offs. Before it became Unisys, Burroughs created Compubur, a joint venture between Burroughs and Mexican capital that manufactures
computers for the Mexican market. In 1985 a former Burroughs general manager left and formed Electrónica Pantera as a joint venture
with a Mexican partner. With 210 production workers, it builds cables and harnesses for the growing Guadalajara computer industry
(Hewlett Packard, IBM, Compubur, Wang, Cherokee) and exports a
small part (2 percent) to the United States. It in turn sources 25
percent of its inputs from Guadalajara, including connectors from
a Canadian-owned manufacturer that also supplies the local IBM

plant but which (at the time of the interview) had not yet qualified to supply local plants of other blue chip electronics firms.

General Instrument generated a spin-off in 1983 when the plant manager left to start Sistemas Delfi, a joint venture with the national telephone company of Mexico, Telmex. With 100 production workers it makes computer keyboards, keys, and printed circuit boards, primarily for Telmex (60 percent of output), but it also does special orders of PCBs and computer keys for Hewlett Packard, IBM, and Unisys. Sistemas Delfi, whose machines were brought from the United States under the maquiladora regimen, exports as a maquiladora when there is excess capacity (but was not doing so at the time of the interview). This spin-off uses 80 percent national inputs for its Telmex products, including 50 percent from Guadalajara—metal and plastic parts, along with gas tubing from General Instrument. Its other clients provide their own raw materials. Productive services such as metal stamping, plastic molding, and tool and die are done in-house.

Services. Four of the six electronics maquiladoras use local tool and die to some degree, covering from a part to all of their needs. Two of the six use local metal stamping, and only one uses local plastic molding. Much of the latter two services still come from the parent company or are done in house. One of the local metal stamping firms used by the foreign electronics plants was started by a former Hewlett Packard engineer. A frequently cited tool and die supplier of the foreign electronics plants, TROMOL (Troquelas y Moldes), is a local company with totally Mexican capital.

The two oldest electronics maquiladoras (which are also the two flexible producers) use local productive services more heavily than do the others. Motorola uses several local productive services: tool and die, metal stamping, plastic molding, and metal plating. It helped create some of these local service providers, brought in a very high tech Japanese metal plating shop, and developed a high quality local tool and die shop, which eventually stopped supplying Motorola and the other maquiladoras because of fluctuations in demand. It now supplies the local internal market. Motorola created some locally owned packaging companies to make dry ice and styrofoam and also developed a chemical plant and electric capacitors plant in Monterrey to supply them. As the manager of the Motorola wafer fabrication plant said, Motorola came here from Nogales to be an integrated manufacturer instead of an assembler.

Foreign Nonmaquiladora Exporters

Unlike the border cities, the electronics industry in Guadalajara is composed of more than just foreign-owned maquiladoras producing for their parent company. There is a sector of large, foreign-owned electronics plants that do not operate as maquiladoras but do export the majority of their output, which is primarily computer-related. IBM initiated the trend in 1981 with a plant that was originally oriented toward the domestic market. As the Mexican market collapsed, however, IBM began exporting more of its output. By 1988 the IBM plant was exporting about four-fifths of the personal computers and memory boards assembled there to forty-four countries in the Pacific Rim (interview, July 1988). Hewlett Packard (1982), Cherokee, Wang (1985), Tandem (1988), and Siemans (Encitel) followed with their own plants. Also in 1988 the existing Kodak plant opened up a new line with one thousand additional employees producing floppy disks and magnetic heads primarily for export and was due to open an automated production line of high density printed circuit boards in 1989.[5]

There is very little buying and selling of products among these wholly owned foreign subsidiaries, whether maquiladora or not, for several reasons. They may not be set up as profit centers and can sell only to their parent company; they may have to send products back to their parent company for testing before they can be sold; in the particular case of maquiladoras, they may not want to deal with the red tape in getting permission to sell locally or they may not need local sales to complement their parent company's demand. The only examples of transactions among the foreign-owned electronics firms we found were Cherokee supplying power supplies to IBM and the Siemans plant (Encitel) providing inputs to Hewlett Packard.

Two of the spin-offs from the electronics maquiladoras have become suppliers to the foreign electronics firms: Electrónica Pantera, which supplies Hewlett Packard, IBM, Compubur, Wang, and Cherokee, and Sistemas Delfi, which supplies Hewlett Packard and IBM (see above). Similar to Sistemas Delfi, Mitel de México, a joint venture between the Canadian Company and Telmex, supplies electronic parts not only to Telmex but also to other electronics firms in Guadalajara.

Both to satisfy local content requirements and have greater just-in-time supplier capabilities, IBM has brought in two captive suppliers from the United States and Hewlett Packard has brought in one. IBM brought in Space Craft Inc. (SCI), which formed a joint venture with the Juárez-based Mexican group ELAMEX to produce high density printed circuit boards with wholly imported inputs. Called Adelantos de Tecnología (ADTEC), the joint venture with 51 percent Mexican capital had wanted to supply IBM from Juárez, but IBM insisted it needed a supplier of sophisticated two-sided PCBs close at hand. ADTEC applied for maquiladora status in order to sell to U.S. buyers in addition to the local IBM plant. However, after landing a contract to supply the local Hewlett Packard plant, ADTEC decided that local demand by the foreign electronics firms was sufficient. Instead, they registered under PITEX to keep open the export option (interviews, July and December 1988). IBM has also brought in another U.S. supplier, Molex, which set up as a wholly owned subsidiary of its U.S. parent company. Hewlett Packard brought in Matsa, which organized as a joint venture, similar to ADTEC.

Endogenous Firms

We identified six endogenous, or locally owned, electronics producers.[6] Only one of these firms has worked itself into the supplier network of the local multinational electronics firms: Instrumentos Electrónicos Profesionales (IEP). IEP sells manually assembled printed circuit boards not only to its Mexican parent company, Mexel, but also to Tandem and Wang. Lack of capital keeps it from expanding into sophisticated surface mount technology as ADTEC and Kodak have.

The remaining endogenous electronics producers, which sell only to domestic firms, include Logix, which was started by a local employee of IBM; Kitron, which is most like a Silicon Valley garage start-up firm; Infor Espacio, which designs and builds computer printers; and Wind, which builds its own brand of computers for the Mexican market. These firms do their own product design, buy the parts (almost totally foreign-made), and assemble them.

Kitron, for example, started up in 1980 with six local partners, four of whom work in the firm. It is a member of the Cámara Nacional de la Industria Eléctrica y Electrónica (CANIECE) and has nearly thirty employees, nine engineers in R&D, ten production workers, four supervisors, and four clerical staff in operations. Kitron designs and assembles digital control instruments. Ten percent of its inputs are domestic—metal housings manufactured in Mexico City. Sixty percent of its inputs are directly imported—integrated circuits and switches. Thirty percent are bought through local distributors although they are manufactured abroad—resistors and connectors. All the engineers were educated in Guadalajara, read English, and follow the industry journals.

Microton, another local electronics start-up, was established in 1979 to design and assemble computer products. The firm imported

80 percent of its raw materials directly and bought the remaining 20 percent through local distributors of foreign-made components. It was not a member of any industry association. In 1982 Microton tried to establish its own line of computers, but government red tape for importing equipment proved to be too complicated. The firm subsequently developed an inexpensive way to build a buffer multiplexor (which allows a computer to be used while its printer works). By December 1988, it was unable to find a firm willing to market its buffer in Mexico and had decided to close up the design and production activities altogether to become simply a computer service and software firm.

While the foreign-based electronics industry in Guadalajara is gradually networking among itself through spin-offs, captive suppliers, and joint ventures, there is a growing endogenous electronics industry that continues to source almost all inputs from abroad. It is almost totally unlinked to the foreign-based electronics industry in Guadalajara.

Auto Parts Network

Four of the five auto parts maquiladoras were established between 1978 and 1981 to manufacture engine, transmission, and brake parts. Three are U.S. subsidiaries and one is a Spanish subsidiary. The only automotive maquiladora built in Guadalajara after the 1982 economic crisis is a Honda plant, established in 1988, which assembles motorcycles. Two of the three U.S. plants are partial maquiladoras, producing primarily for the Mexican market and exporting to the United States as excess capacity warrants. The Spanish plant, which sells exclusively to Europe, is applying for permission to sell a portion to the domestic market. Honda has permission to sell 10 percent of its output in the domestic market. The rest goes to the U.S. market. These plants are small, ranging from 25 to 125 production workers. The use of female workers varies considerably, from only 2 percent in the Honda plant to 75 percent in one of the U.S. plants. Only one of the plants, a Borg Warner plant, reported a substantial use of temporary workers (25 percent). This plant uses 60 percent women line workers.

The auto parts maquiladoras cite the existence of the local metal mechanics industry as an important location factor for both inputs and experienced labor force. In fact, the local productive inputs they use come mainly from this sector: metal casting boxes, metal ball bearings and pellets, brass, nails, and cutting tools, plus solvent and paints. Nevertheless, the plants do not use much of these inputs.

The use of local inputs, which varies from 0 to 10 percent for the five plants, averages only slightly higher than that for the electronics plants (see Table 16). Two out of the five use local tool and die services and two use local metal stamping. Only one of the firms, Honda, reports any significant use of local subcontracting (and just to a moderate degree).[7]

Unlike the electronics plants, the auto parts maquiladoras use substantial inputs from elsewhere in Mexico, averaging 37 percent of total inputs (see Table 16). Far from its parent company, the Spanish plant gets a major part of it solvents and paints from Mexico City, Puebla, and Monterrey. One of the U.S. plants that is a partial maquiladora gets its main input, steel, from Monterrey and Mexico City. Other domestic inputs from outside Guadalajara include rivets, ball bearings, steel bars and plates from Monterrey and Mexico City.

Borg Warner opened its first plant in Guadalajara in 1978, called Industria de Repuestos. It produces rings for car engines and pillow blocks for transmissions, using a substantial degree of computer-controlled production machines. It is the third flexible producer identified among the maquiladoras in Guadalajara, along with Motorola and Unisys.

Industria de Repuestos is a partial maquiladora, exporting 15 percent of its output (primarily rings) to the United States. In 1980 Borg Warner opened another branch plant, BW Componentes. This one is a total maquiladora producing time chains for car engines for its parent company in the United States.

The Spanish plant, Renza (Elementos de Freno), currently gets its metal stamping from Italy and Spain but is planning to open a metal-stamping factory in Guadalajara for easier access. Renza has also applied to sell 5 to 10 percent of its output domestically, primarily in Guadalajara.

Other

The appliance firm is of note (see Table 16) because of its high percent of local inputs. Belonging to Krups, the German home appliance manufacturer, this plant is the exception for foreign-owned maquiladoras in terms of its high degree of local sourcing. Opened in December 1988, the plant uses plastic inputs from Guadalajara, glass from Monterrey, metal from the United States, and electric motors from Germany. Labor represents only 10 percent of its total costs, and access to raw materials is cited as a major location factor in coming to Guadalajara, along with low turnover rates and skilled labor. The Krups firm, which in 1989 employed only twenty-four workers (all skilled), planned to be at capacity in 1991.

The U.S.-owned plastics firm is of note because of the startlingly high use of national inputs—96 percent. The plant, which manufactures plastic tablecloths, gets its major input, plastic resin, from Mexico City and Puebla (coming originally from the petrochemical complex in Tampico).

A Comparison with Monterrey

Monterrey is a city of heavier industry and more conflictive labor relations than Guadalajara. It is Mexico's second largest industrial city and the leading producer of metal and glass for the internal market. Monterrey's leading *grupos,* or locally owned industrial conglomerates, were greatly affected by the crisis of 1982, the dismantling of tariff protections accompanying Mexico's membership in GATT, and the decline of the internal market. By 1983 the unemployment rate for Monterrey had reached 11.5 percent, more than twice the 1980 rate of 5.5 percent. In 1986 the state of Nuevo León began to promote maquiladoras to absorb the unemployed labor created by the decline in domestic industry. There were three registered maquiladoras in 1986, eighteen in 1987, fifty-eight in 1988, and seventy-three in 1989, of which about 60 percent were located in Monterrey. Nevertheless, the unemployment rate in February 1989 was down only to 10 percent. As a point of comparison with the Guadalajara findings, fifteen out of thirty-four (44 percent) maquiladoras were surveyed in Monterrey.[8]

The high local content in Monterrey's maquiladora products (see Table 17) does not mean that Monterrey is creating new local manufacturing capacity to supply foreign-initiated export activity. Rather, the high local content reflects in great part the successful efforts of some of Monterrey's local *grupos* to adapt to the new milieu by using excess capacity for the export market. Thus the maquiladoras associated with a local *grupo* average 32 percent of local content, while the independent foreign subsidiaries average only 5 percent.

Put in another way, five of the top six maquiladoras in terms of local content are associated with a local *grupo* (see Appendix 4). Two of the five are majority owned by longstanding local *grupos* who were restructuring toward the export market by adding maquiladora operations. One is operated by a local *grupo* who restructured by seeking a foreign buyout. The remaining two are joint ventures, with the local *grupo* holding the minority share. One of these joint ventures existed before becoming a maquiladora in 1986.[9]

Table 17 *Characteristics of Monterrey's Maquiladoras by Sector, 1988–1989*

Sector	No. of Plants	Average % Local Inputs	Average % Natl. Inputs	% Foreign-owned	Year Established (average)	Average No. of Workers	Average % Female	Average Training (wks.)
Associated with local *grupo*	8	32	39	75	1985	181	41	7
Glass	1	100	100	100	1987	60	0	8
Metal	3	34	53	100	1984	286	0	5
Food	2	25	25	0	1983	100	85	12
Electric/electronics	2	0	0	100	1986	167	78	3
Independent	7	5	6	100	1987	202	76	4
Electronics	2	0	0	100	1988	249	93	4
Auto Parts	1	10	20	100	1986	60	50	8
Other	4	6	6	100	1986	216	75	3

Source: Wilson survey, 1988–1989.

Besides being associated with a local *grupo*, the top firms in terms of local content are manufacturers as opposed to pure assembly plants. All seven of the surveyed firms that reported some local content are classified as mass production manufacturers (see Appendix 4). These seven maquiladoras, therefore, show high degrees of manufacturing versus assembly and little or no use of computer-controlled production machinery. Because of the high value added in these top seven manufacturing firms, four of them do not qualify for 806/807 tariff preferences in entering the goods into the United States. Three of these plants enter the goods duty-free into the United States under GSP, which requires 35 percent domestic (i.e., Mexican) content. Another plant uses 806/807 only for some of its product lines. Reflecting the high value-added manufacturing, labor costs represent less than 14 percent of total costs for these firms, compared to the remaining maquiladoras surveyed in Monterrey, whose labor costs average 47 percent of total costs.

The high usage of temporary workers in these plants reflects the striking difference in labor relations between Guadalajara and Monterrey. The heightened industrial working-class consciousness and unionization in Monterrey compared to Guadalajara led the local *grupos* to restructure not only by looking for export markets but also by reducing labor costs through the hiring of temporary workers with little job security and low benefits.

Sectorally, most of these seven plants represent Monterrey's leading industrial sectors—metal (three plants), glass (one plant), and citrus processing (one plant). One of these seven firms sources all its inputs locally: A joint venture with a local *grupo*, it manufactures glass table tops using local glass, chemicals, and packaging material, all for export to the United States.

The main locally manufactured productive inputs that these seven firms buy are glass, laminated steel, galvanized steel, aluminum finishing stock, iron castings, copper wire, paint, chemicals, insulation material, and orange juice. Several also get packaging material, including cardboard cartons and plastic bags, and wooden pallets. One firm, however, said it no longer sources laminated steel bearings, steel bars, or copper wire locally because the exchange rate with the dollar has made them too expensive. It now sources these items from the United States.

The use of local services among the maquiladoras is surprisingly limited, compared to Guadalajara. Of the top seven plants, only four of them use local producer services, mainly tool and die. One uses some local plastic molding, although most of its plastic molding is done in the United States. One uses local painting and metal stamping. Several said that the exchange rate now makes local services (and some raw materials) too expensive.

The eight plants with no local or national content use even fewer local productive services. The three flexible producers, two of which are in electronics, utilize no local inputs other than packaging material such as boxes and plastic bags. Of the remaining five plants with no local productive inputs, only one uses local tool and die, one uses local plastic molding, and two use local packaging materials. None uses any national productive inputs.

The motivation for maquiladoras unassociated with local *grupos* to locate in Monterrey does not hinge on the availability of local inputs. One electronics plant relocated here from the border because of higher labor turnover rates at the border. Mattel, which has a plant in Tijuana, opened one in Monterrey because of better schooling and work ethic, availability of technical personnel, and a labor cost that the company found to be 13 percent lower than at the border—an important consideration for their very labor intensive production process.

Local spin-offs are not happening in Monterrey nearly to the degree that they are happening in Guadalajara. Of the fifteen plants surveyed we identified only one case, where one of the Carrier plants (Elizondo #1) created another plant (Elizondo #3) for low volume, short batch production of air-conditioning parts for both export and the internal market. We did discover two unusual spin-offs to the Texas border: Two of the plants created their own U.S. parent companies, although with 100 percent Mexican capital, locating "headquarters" in a warehouse in Laredo in one case and McAllen in the other case.

One incipient domestic linkage detected by the transaction analysis, however, is that between the foreign-owned electronics maquiladoras of Monterrey and the growing foreign-dominated electronics network in Guadalajara. There is an expanding network of trade among foreign-owned electronics firms in Mexico. Two of the Monterrey maquiladoras, both subsidiaries of U.S. firms, have applied for and been approved to sell up to 20 percent of their product on the internal market in order to participate in this growing electronics trade network: American Electric and Rogers Electronics. Rogers Electronics is starting to sell to IBM and Hewlett Packard in Guadalajara.[10]

A Comparison with the Border

Thirty border plants—ten each from Tijuana, Juárez, and Nuevo Laredo—were interviewed, representing 2.7 percent of all border plants.

The border maquiladoras generate very few local linkages. Only one maquiladora out of the thirty surveyed reports any local inputs: Located in Tijuana, it is a sporting goods plant manufacturing wooden oars for its parent company in Los Angeles. It uses sandpaper and varnish made in Tijuana.

Five of the thirty border plants interviewed indicate some use of nonlocal national inputs. Three are in Tijuana and two in Nuevo Laredo. The Japanese home appliance manufacturer Sanyo, which manufacturers and assembles vacuum cleaners in Tijuana, buys resins and motor ventilators manufactured in Mexico City and the state of México. While it has the greatest use of national inputs among the border maquiladoras interviewed, it is not a pure maquiladora. Sanyo sells 40 percent of its output on the internal market. Another Japanese company in Tijuana with national inputs manufactures and assembles electric transformers and coils. It brings in its main inputs—laminated steel and copper wire—from the United States but buys Mexican-made alcohol, glue, tools, and argon gas from distributors in Tijuana. The third company in Tijuana with national inputs is the sporting goods manufacturer, which uses unspecified minor inputs from Guadalajara and Monterrey.

One of the two plants with nonlocal domestic content in Nuevo Laredo repairs, laminates, and converts cars. Owned by a Mexican American from Laredo, the company buys Mexican-made paints from a distributor in Nuevo Laredo and cleaners made in Monterrey. However, its principal inputs of wood and resin come from the United States. A U.S.-owned shoe plant that assembles moccasins in Nuevo Laredo sources a small percentage of its leather from León, Guanajuato.

Unlike in Guadalajara, there are few partial maquiladoras along the border. In fact, the only one in our sample is the Sanyo plant in Tijuana, which produces 40 percent of its output for the Mexican market. Of the maquiladora production, 55 percent goes to the United States and 45 percent to other countries, including Canada, Panama, and Asia (Japan, Hong Kong, and Malaysia).

Very few border maquiladoras use productive services from the Mexican side or from the U.S. twin city, except in Tijuana. The most frequently used local productive service is tool and die, with four of the ten Tijuana plants using occasional local tool and die services, one of ten Nuevo Laredo firms, and none of the Juárez firms. Most of the plants needing tool and die services get them in the United States (nonborder). Of the thirteen plants reporting the use of metal-stamping services, almost all source this service in the United States as well, including Japanese firms. One Japanese firm sources it in Japan and another Japanese plant does some of it in-house as well as sourcing from both the United States and Japan. Only one firm—a U.S. assembler of switches for automobiles in Juárez—reported sourcing metal stamping in its twin city of El Paso.

Plastic molding—both extrusions and injection molding—is used by sixteen (over half) of the maquiladoras surveyed along the border. All the U.S.-owned plants reported getting their plastic molding from the United States (nonborder) except two: the automobile switch assembly plant in Juárez, which gets its plastic molding along with metal stamping in El Paso, and an electronics plant in Tijuana, which gets it from Singapore.

Among the Japanese plants in Tijuana, there is an interesting trend going on in plastic molding. Some maquiladoras continue to source plastic molding from Japan, while some have substituted those imports with their own in-house plastic molding and others have brought captive suppliers over from Japan, who then diversify their maquiladora clients. In our sample of five Japanese maquiladoras in Tijuana,[11] two still bring their plastic molding from Japan and one does it in-house. Another, Sanyo, does part of it in-house and gets part from a Japanese supplier, Mutsutech, which Sanyo brought over as a captive supplier from Japan. Mutsutech set up as a maquiladora that sells all of its output in the foreign trade zone in Tijuana to other maquiladoras—not only Sanyo now, but also Matsuchita and Hitachi. Mutsutech, in turn, imports all of its inputs from Japan and the United States. Another Japanese plant has developed a local supplier relationship with a plastic-molding company in Otay, California.[12] In 1988 the Sony plant in Piedras Negras[13] began to manufacture its own plastic cassette holders with robotic machines brought from Japan, after having imported cassette holders manufactured in Japan by Sanyo.

The role of the twin cities in the border maquiladoras' transactions networks is quite limited, primarily to nonproductive services. In terms of productive inputs produced in the twin cities, the survey found one Tijuana maquiladora buying tools made in the San Diego area, another Tijuana plant buying resin from the San Diego area, and a Juárez company buying tools and oil from El Paso. In terms of twin city productive services, the survey found the one Japanese company in Tijuana sourcing plastic molding in Otay and one Juárez company sourcing plastic extrusion and metal stamping in El Paso.

None of the thirty border respondents reported any local spin-offs from their plants.

Conclusions

This analysis of transaction networks reveals two major findings. First, the relatively high percent of Mexican inputs—local and national—used by the maquiladoras of the interior is not a result of foreign investment creating enough demand to stimulate a local supplier industry; rather, it is the result primarily of local capital seeking to survive by looking for export markets through maquiladora status. Local producers, as they become maquiladoras, continue to use some of their local supplier networks for inputs. In contrast, foreign-owned and -initiated maquiladoras, like those that typify the border region, continue on the whole to rely almost exclusively on imported inputs.

Second, the firms with the greatest local content are not the second generation flexible producers but rather manufacturers and assemblers. In the case of Guadalajara, the maquiladoras with greatest local inputs are part of the endogenous crafts sector—mainly small, locally owned plants producing shoes, clothing, furniture, jewelry, and toys. Most continue to sell on the internal market but export to U.S. clients as excess capacity warrants. In Monterrey, the maquiladoras with greatest local inputs were initiated primarily by the leading local industrial families, or *grupos*, in an attempt to survive the decline of the domestic market by seeking U.S. clients, joint ventures, or even buyouts. In both locations, local content in these maquiladora operations still consists of minor inputs and is less than in their counterpart domestic operations.

The foreign-owned and -initiated maquiladoras remain largely integrated to their U.S. supplier networks, despite the interior location. Even in Guadalajara, the plant managers claim they maintain just-in-time inventories with U.S.-based providers. Despite the few local (or national) inputs used by the foreign-owned maquiladoras in Guadalajara, there is nonetheless a developing local transactional network involving the foreign-owned electronics firms. The older ones especially have established joint ventures, created spin-offs, brought in outside suppliers, and worked with a few local service providers. There is now a nationally recognized electronics market in Guadalajara. The emerging network, however, excludes almost all the small endogenous electronics firms.

In Monterrey the foreign-initiated maquiladoras that are unassociated with local *grupos* have located there to escape the high labor turnover rates of the border and have access to an industrial milieu along with urban amenities, but not because of access to local raw materials. They have established very few local linkages in terms of inputs, services, or spin-off firms.

In the interior as well as the border, the flexible producers use fewer domestic inputs than average (see chapter 4). In Guadalajara, nevertheless, the three maquiladoras evidencing flexible production methods use somewhat more domestic inputs than do the other foreign maquiladoras. This fact could be explained by the age of the maquiladoras in two of the cases: They are both over twenty years old. In the other case, it could be explained by the sector: Auto parts maquiladoras in Guadalajara use locally manufactured metal mechanic inputs as well as significant national inputs from both Mexico City and Monterrey. In Monterrey most of the domestic content is accounted for by mass production manufacturers. In Guadalajara the use of domestic inputs is split more evenly between manufacturers and labor-intensive assembly plants (with emphasis on the former), reflecting the mixed classifications of the craft-producing maquiladoras.

The border plants are still largely appendages of the U.S. firms without much local networking. The main exception is the Japanese plants in Tijuana, which are bringing in captive suppliers as a local source of some inputs and manufacturing other inputs themselves. The heralded anecdotes about U.S. border maquiladoras bringing in captive suppliers did not show up in this survey.

6. From Motorola to Mextron: Case Studies of Individual Business Strategies

Sectoral and geographic analysis of maquiladoras integrates the fascinating stories of many individual firms into a coherent whole. But the individual stories themselves transmit a more tangible realistic sense of the frustrations and challenges facing the maquiladoras. For public policy making, an appreciation of these individual experiences is vital. The following vignettes are offered, drawing on the interviews with those managers and owners who did not request anonymity for their firm.[1] From Guadalajara, six locally owned maquiladoras are portrayed and five foreign-owned maquiladoras. From Monterrey, four maquiladoras owned in part at least by local conglomerates are profiled, along with three plants that are totally foreign-owned. For the border, two plants from Juárez, three from Nuevo Laredo, and four from Tijuana are described.

Locally Owned Plants in Guadalajara

The strategies of the small and medium-sized local manufacturers for coping with the decline of the internal market since 1982 are varied. Many tried maquiladora status but gave up in disgust because of the uncertainties of demand from the principal client. Our survey contains all those that have kept some version of a maquiladora strategy. For a selection of these locally owned producers, we recount here their coping strategy, as best we could determine it from the interview, and describe their choices in technology and management methods, their sourcing and marketing strategies, plus their views of a Guadalajara location vis-à-vis a border location.

Industrias Pinfer, SA (Footwear)

For Industrias Pinfer a successful coping strategy entailed not only becoming a maquiladora but selling out to its principal U.S. client.

Having opened the plant in 1986 well after the crisis in the internal market had begun, the owner, a long-time Guadalajaran resident, had planned from the beginning to enter the U.S. market in addition to selling to the flagging internal market. Nevertheless, he found it much easier to sell to local retail shoe chains, which he did right from the start, than to export to the United States. It took him little time to realize that the easiest access to the external market was through maquiladora status, since the client would provide inputs, machinery, and a market. Within two years Industrias Pinfer became a maquiladora, producing for a single U.S. client in Puerto Rico.

Now with $450,000 worth of machinery and equipment and 120 line workers (60 percent female), sales to the U.S. client occupy 98 percent of total output, the remainder being sold domestically. The demand for output by the U.S. client is growing. The owner finally decided that the best way to expand is by being bought out by the U.S. client firm. At the time of the interview, the U.S. client had agreed to buy out a majority share of the firm and to finance the plant's expansion. Thus this personal success story in profitably adapting to the new economic conditions will mean one less locally owned company for Guadalajara with less use of local inputs than if it had been able to survive in the domestic market or export on its own to the United States.

Industrias Pinfer performs an unusual maquila function for its overseas client: cutting the shoe material, rather than stitching the cut pieces together. Forty percent of the line workers are skilled. Nevertheless, the operation is still labor intensive, with wages and salaries accounting for the majority (60 percent) of total production costs. There are no computerized machines. The owner is implementing a few of the soft aspects of flexible technology: involving the workers to a small degree in problem diagnosis, machinery maintenance, and continuous quality control.

The main productive inputs come from the United States—Milwaukee, Houston, and New Hampshire. Some minor inputs (accounting for 20 percent of the total) are sourced in Guadalajara: glues, thread, tapes, and tacks. Most tool and die work is done locally, although metal stamping is done in the United States.

The management sees the labor situation in Guadalajara and this plant (where the workers belong to the largest Mexican manufacturing union, CTM) as without problem. While the initial reason for locating in Guadalajara was the fact that the owners lived there, they would invest again in Guadalajara if they had to make the decision again.

Industrial Ratana, SA (Furniture)

This small manufacturer, making chairs and sofas for offices, opened in 1987 intending to sell to the domestic market. The owner found not only a tight market but also rapidly soaring prices of key domestic inputs. He sought maquiladora status in order to escape inflationary input prices in Mexico, since maquiladora clients typically provide most of the raw materials. After getting sufficient contract offers, the firm converted totally to maquiladora status in 1988.

Industrial Ratana has only twelve line workers, seven of which are women. Using U.S. Tariff Codes 806/807, the firm exports all of its output to clients in the United States, from where it gets its primary inputs of cloth, polyurethane, and forged metal. Some minor inputs (accounting for 20 percent of the total) come from Guadalajara—primarily solder, screws, staples, glues, and tape. The owner, who has a university education, said that no productive services were sourced locally, although metal stamping came from Naucalpan in the state of México.

The production process is labor intensive (45 percent of production costs are for labor) and involves no computer-controlled production machinery. Nevertheless, the owner has implemented some of the soft aspects of flexible production: continuous quality control, quality circles, and SPC.

The owner said that the only labor problem he encountered in Guadalajara was difficulty in finding specialized technicians. His workers are not unionized. He would locate again in Guadalajara if he had to make the decision again.

Joyería y Diseños Gonzales, SA (Jewelry)

This family-run jewelry manufacturing firm has not done well as a maquiladora in Guadalajara. Originally established in 1985 to produce for the domestic market, the owners soon realized they needed access to the U.S. market and more capital. They took on a Los Angeles–based firm as a minority partner (20 percent) and began to produce as a maquiladora for them. However, the Los Angeles firm also contracted with another maquiladora in Juárez to produce the same things, thus pitting the two against each other. The Gonzales family sees the Juárez maquiladora as their biggest competitor. They estimate that labor productivity (output per worker per hour) is the same in both plants, but the distance from Guadalajara to the border creates a real competitive disadvantage for them. If they could make the decision again, they would remain a maquiladora but move their plant to the border, despite Guadalajara's lower turnover rates, good labor climate, and the fact that the workers in this plant are not unionized.

With $15,000 invested in machinery and equipment and twenty-eight line workers, 86 percent of which are women, the firm makes gold chains, rings, and earrings. Joyería y Diseños Gonzales gets almost all the main inputs—gold, bronze, and molds—from the Los Angeles firm and a small amount from Mexico City. Industrial gases are the only locally produced input. Even plastic injection molding and metal stamping are done in Los Angeles. All the products reenter the United States under TC 806/807.

The production process is labor intensive, although it involves value-added manufacturing. The firm does not use computer-controlled production machines, nor JIT, nor SPC. Nevertheless, it does use worker participation in problem diagnosis, continuous quality control, and quality circles.

Huramex (Footwear)

This leather shoe manufacturer became a maquiladora in 1988 after only one year of producing exclusively for the internal market and also took on its main U.S. client as a minority partner (10 percent). However, the difference with the jewelry manufacturer is that it did not become totally dependent on the one client. Only one-third of its sales are to the U.S. client/partner using maquiladora status and TC 806/807.

The U.S. client provides the major input—leather—in the form of cut leather components. The fifteen women on the maquiladora line at Huramex stitch the components together. Only glues and thread are sourced locally (the glues come from a local plant of the 3M Corporation). Even plastic injection molding comes from the United States (Indio, California). The management reported that distance to the U.S. border was a disadvantage for their maquiladora operations, but with the good labor climate (the workers in this plant belong to the CROC, a local union), they would put their plant in Guadalajara again if they had to decide again.

The domestic operations, which account for two-thirds of sales, involve twenty-five workers—all women—in the entire shoe-manufacturing process, including cutting as well as stitching. The leather for the domestic operations comes from León, Guanajuato. In addition to thread and glues manufactured in Guadalajara, the domestic operations use locally made accessories and tacks. About a fourth of their domestic production is sold to a shoe company in Guadalajara.

The management considers the plant to be more of a manufacturing than an assembly operation. It uses traditional labor-intensive technology with no computer-controlled machines, nor JIT. Management employs a small degree of worker participation in problem diagnosis and quality control, along with a small degree of SPC. The production manager claimed that the plant does use a system of continuous quality control.

Artículos de Piel de Guadalajara (Clothing)

This leather clothing company, which began producing for the internal market in 1988, also changed rapidly to maquiladora status but kept the maquiladora production to only 20 percent of total sales. It also kept the ownership entirely local. Of the company's twenty-six blue collar workers, eight—all women—work in the maquiladora operation. The leather is cut in the United States, stitched in Guadalajara, and finished in the United States. The main input, leather components, comes from the United States, with only thread and glues sourced locally. Of the domestic production, about 40 percent is sold to local department stores in Guadalajara. This firm is one of the few locally owned maquiladoras to use a sizable portion of temporary employees—20 percent. It was also the only one whose manager complained about the lack of training and skills of the line workers and, in fact, because of this problem he was unsure whether or not they would locate in Guadalajara if they could make the decision again. He had no complaints, however, about the union to which the workers belong (CTM, the largest Mexican union). The manager characterized the operation as manufacturing, rather than assembly, yet a labor-intensive operation employing traditional technology and management methods. Twenty thousand dollars has been invested in machinery and equipment.

Furnimex, SA (Furniture)

This water-bed manufacturer opened directly as a maquiladora in 1987, with 80 percent local capital and 20 percent capital from the U.S. client/partner in Mattapoisets, Massachusetts. The initial investment in machinery and equipment was about $25,000. The U.S. partners have no other maquiladora or U.S. plant producing waterbeds. Their reason for seeking a maquiladora in Guadalajara was the local availability of inputs, primarily wood. All their wood and glues come from Guadalajara. All their paints and varnishes and metal stampings come from elsewhere in Mexico. Thus 30 percent of their inputs are from Guadalajara and 20 percent from elsewhere in Mexico. The plastic vinyl cloth, which accounts for 50 percent of the productive inputs, comes from Massachusetts, as do molded plastic pieces. Even with a total of 50 percent domestic content, the water beds enter the United States with full benefit of TC 806/807.

Another reason for establishing a maquiladora in Guadalajara was to avoid the high labor turnover rates among the maquiladoras along the border. The owners have been pleased with the labor situation in Guadalajara in terms of both quality and stability. The forty-three line workers—a fourth of whom are women—belong to the largest Mexican union (CTM). They have had one strike, which was over wages.

The management finds good communication links with Massachusetts. Although the distance is inconvenient, they would not locate elsewhere if they were to make the decision again.

The management characterizes the operation as manufacturing, rather than assembly, yet with fairly traditional labor intensive technology, including no use of computer-controlled production machines. The management does utilize, however, a moderate degree of worker participation in problem diagnosis and continuous quality control and uses quality circles and SPC, but not JIT.

Foreign-Owned Plants in Guadalajara

Some of the large foreign-owned maquiladoras in Guadalajara have adopted second generation flexible technology and others have not; some have taken on value-added manufacturing, while others have remained labor intensive assembly operations; some have sought local suppliers, some have brought U.S. suppliers to Guadalajara, and others continue to use suppliers in the United States. Some of the newer foreign-owned plants have come to Guadalajara to escape the high labor turnover rates along the border; others have come to take advantage of the availability of local inputs. The following selections exemplify these different strategies.

Motorola Semiconductores

This maquiladora, wholly owned by Motorola Semiconductors in Phoenix, Arizona, began in 1969 as a labor intensive electronic assembly operation. Nevertheless, in 1985 it began upgrading its machinery, introducing technology from Motorola's plants in Austin and Phoenix, including computer-controlled production machines. It also began manufacturing wafers and chips rather than just assembling them.

The general manager, a Mexican national, said that being in Guadalajara rather than the border allowed it to become an integrated manufacturing plant because of the availability of good engineers and technicians and the well-developed local industrial base. In fact, wafer fabrication was moved to Guadalajara from a plant in Nogales because of the lack of a manufacturing base and technical personnel at the border. Nevertheless, he said, distance to U.S. and European suppliers, where all the chip parts come from, is a problem, and JIT inventorying on inputs from abroad cannot be maintained.[2]

Taking advantage of the local industrial base, Motorola has been one of the most aggressive foreign maquiladoras in Guadalajara to establish a local supplier network—not of chip parts, but of producer services and packaging materials. Motorola uses local tool and die, metal stamping, plastic molding, and metal plating. It developed a high quality local tool and die shop, which now supplies other local producers. It brought in a very high tech Japanese metal-plating shop. Motorola created some locally owned packaging companies to make dry ice and styrofoam. Motorola has also developed some domestic suppliers of productive inputs: a chemical plant and an electric capacitors plant in Monterrey. The only productive input manufactured in Guadalajara is industrial gases from the local Union Carbide plant. Total domestic content in terms of productive inputs is less than 5 percent.

The general manager characterized the labor situation in Guadalajara as calm, and turnover rates very low, especially compared to the border. None of Motorola's nearly 2,500 line workers is unionized, none are temporary workers, and the firm does not subcontract. The workers have been gradually adapting to the use of flexible production methods on the shop floor such as JIT, SPC, and quality circles. In fact, the general manager, in comparing his workers' productivity to Motorola's parallel plant in the United States, said that his workers had greater productivity with similar technology mainly because of their level of dedication to the work process. He characterized the productivity with Motorola's parallel plant in France as about the same, but said that the parallel plant in the Far East was more productive because it was more automated. He said, though, that they were in the process of bringing in more state-of-the-art machinery to the Guadalajara plant.

The plant's market has been changing over time, with now less than half of the output going to the United States, a large part going to the Far East, some to Europe, and less than 5 percent to Mexico (Motorola was the first foreign maquiladora to be authorized in domestic sales). Since the semiconductors going to the United States are already tax-exempt, they do not receive 806/807 duty exemptions. The Motorola plant sells about 1 percent of its output in Guadalajara through three distributors. It does not sell to Unisys, IBM, or other semiconductor users in Guadalajara because its output goes back to Motorola's U.S., European, or Far Eastern plants for final inspection. The general manager also expressed the fear that a lot of red tape would be involved in selling to other maquiladoras in Guadalajara.

Unisys (formerly Burroughs)

The Burroughs maquiladora was established in 1968 to assemble cables, harnesses, and power supplies for the parent company in the United States.[3] The plant was closed in 1991 during a worldwide restructuring. In the mid-1980s Burroughs began introducing computer-controlled production machinery, just-in-time inventorying (with inputs as well as in-process stocks), continuous quality control, quality circles, multiskilling, and, starting in 1988 at about the time of the Unisys merger, statistical process control. The management was very pleased with the production workers' skills, education level (almost all had completed high school), adaptability to the new methods, and company loyalty. Nevertheless, the management complained that their worker productivity was only about 80 percent as high as in Unisys' parallel plants, even taking into account lower labor costs, because of downtime from spare part delays from the Unisys plant in Dallas.

Unisys' 800 line workers, 80 percent of which were women, belonged to the predominant union, CTM. A quarter of the workers were temporaries, which was high compared to locally owned maquiladoras.

Unisys did more than any of the foreign electronics maquiladoras in Guadalajara to develop a domestic supplier base. According to the procurement director, the plant sourced 12 percent of its productive inputs domestically, including some of its terminals and connectors, metal parts, and cables. This was a very high percentage for a foreign electronics maquiladora. Only a small portion of the domestic productive inputs was manufactured in Guadalajara: metal parts (chassis). In 1989 the company was developing two new suppliers elsewhere in Mexico that would manufacture cables and connectors with 50 percent domestic content. The Unisys plant also used local productive service providers. The plant designed its own tooling in-house but contracted with five local tool and die makers for the fabrication. Nevertheless, the management complained that spare machine parts were hard to get locally and sometimes hard to get in a timely manner from Dallas. Unisys created two spin-off firms, Compubur and Electrónica Pantera (see chapter 4), that are much more integrated into the Guadalajara electronics industry in terms of local inputs and sales.

Communications and transportation logistics with the United States were crucial to the plant's operations. All the plant's output went back to the United States, primarily to the Dallas plant, mostly by truck (95 percent) and the rest by air (5 percent). The management considered the transportation linkages with the United States to be adequate in terms of truck transportation and commercial air flights. While it also considered computer link-ups with the United States to be adequate, it was considering buying a communications satellite. The main advantage to being located in Guadalajara as opposed to the border was availability of skilled engineers. In fact, the plant began to "export" engineers to the Dallas plant and the Canadian plant. The management also considered labor turnover rates and living conditions for management to be more attractive in Guadalajara than at the border.

General Instrument

General Instrument established a Guadalajara maquiladora in 1974 after six years of operating on the border at Nogales. In the 1980s the parent company opted not to put much effort in introducing second generation flexible production methods in the Guadalajara plant. As a result, the plant remains a traditional labor intensive electronics assembly operation. Worker productivity is lower than at the company's parallel plant in Belgium. At the time of the interview in 1989, General Instrument was considering selling the plant. Later that year it was bought by C. P. Clare, a Chicago-based marketing firm.

According to the production manager, the plant has almost no computer-controlled production machinery, no JIT, and no use of flexible work relations such as multiskilling or quality circles. The management is introducing some computerized SPC and a continuous quality control program called AQL (acceptable quality level). Using traditional technology, the plant still has the flexibility to do small batches of less than one hour of production time on traditional labor intensive products (electronic voltage surge suppressors and relays). On average there are four design changes each day, utilizing the labor intensive technology.

General Instrument moved its maquiladora from Nogales to Guadalajara, not to create an integrated manufacturing operation, as with Motorola, but to escape the high turnover rates and low education levels of the blue-collar labor force at the border. The company's expectations were fulfilled. Almost all of the 500 line workers in the Guadalajara plant—90 percent of which are women—have completed high school. The turnover rate is low. In general, the management finds the labor climate in Guadalajara to be good. The CTM has caused them few problems.

The main drawback with the Guadalajara location is the distance to the United States. The plant gets much of its productive inputs and services from the parent company plants in the United States and sells most of its output (85 percent) to parent company plants in the United States. The plant also sources substantial inputs from Japan and Belgium and sells 10 percent of its output to Belgium. The nearby Pacific port of Manzanilla has been adequate for most of the company's shipping needs, except that getting goods through customs is sometimes slow.

The plant has received permission from the Mexican government to sell a part of its output on the domestic market. It sells gas tubing, accounting for 5 percent of sales, to a local spin-off firm started in 1983 by the former General Instrument plant manager (see chapter 4).

The plant does not source any productive inputs or services from Mexico. Plastic injection molding comes from Belgium and the United States. Metal stamping is done in the United States. Tool and die work is done in-house. The management reports it has been unable to find good local suppliers but is talking to IBM about some of its local suppliers, most of whom IBM has brought in from the United States (see chapter 4).

Krups

This maquiladora, started by the German home appliance maker in 1989 to manufacture coffeemakers and toasters for the U.S. market, has the highest degree of locally manufactured inputs of any of the foreign maquiladoras in Guadalajara (30 percent). This high use of local inputs comes from the purchase of all its plastic parts in Guadalajara. It also buys glass parts made in Monterrey, for a total domestic content of 35 percent. Metal comes from the United States and motors and transformers from Germany.[4]

The management characterizes the operation as predominantly capital intensive manufacturing, rather than labor intensive assembly. Labor costs account for only 10 percent of total production costs, with raw materials accounting for 75 percent. Traditional noncomputerized production technology is used. Nevertheless, the management has implemented continuous quality control, SPC, and worker participation in problem diagnosis, quality control, and quality circles. The plant is similar in technology and management methods to the company's parallel plants in Ireland and Hong Kong and has similar worker productivity as well.

Despite the need to be near the U.S. market, the management finds Guadalajara a better site than the border because of better access to inputs, lower labor turnover, and higher skill levels of the line workers.[5] Moreover, the management considers communication and transportation from Guadalajara to foreign markets and suppliers to be adequate.

Tulon

Tulon, Inc., of Gardena, California (a division of Easterline), abandoned its Tijuana maquiladora and opened the Guadalajara plant in 1985 to make circuit board drills for the parent company.[6] Like General Instrument, Tulon opted not to invest in flexible technology. The general manager said the machinery is ten years behind the automated equipment used in the parallel plant in Gardena. The plant has a traditional quality control department, although the management has begun to introduce some continuous quality control methods and worker participation in quality control. The plant does not use SPC, nor does it crosstrain workers to become multiskilled for assignment rotation.

Unlike General Instrument, Tulon made its Guadalajara plant primarily a manufacturing rather than assembly operation. Of the 100 line workers, 85 percent are men. The work is heavier, dirtier, and requires more training than at the Tijuana plant, according to the general manager. In fact, Tulon abandoned its Tijuana plant not only to escape the high labor turnover rates, but to gain access to a labor force that is more suited to manufacturing. The general manager has been pleased not only with the availability of locally trained engineers and technicians such as mechanics and machinists, but also with the unskilled workers, who show a strong work ethic, company loyalty, and adaptability to the work process. The management has had some "problems" with the CTM, the union to which the workers belong. There have also been attendance problems with the line workers. Nevertheless the quality, availability, and adaptability of the line workers has been a strong attraction compared to the border. The general manager also cited the availability of good quality local tool and die as a major attraction of Guadalajara.

The distance from the United States is not perceived as a problem for the Guadalajara plant. According to the general manager, it is easier to fly supplies in here from the plant's three major providers in Boston, New Jersey, and Japan than it was to truck the goods in to the border. Also maritime shipping is actually easier from Guadalajara than Tijuana because the port of Manzanilla is less busy than the port of San Diego. Rail links to Guadalajara are very unfavorable compared to the border, said the general manager, but his plant does not need to use them much. The main communications problem is telephone.

The general manager finds JIT impossible at his Guadalajara plant not because of the distance, but because he cannot depend on the parent company getting supplies and replacement parts to him on time. Thus the plant maintains a six-month inventory of inputs. Almost all (96 percent) of the plant's productive inputs come from the United States or Japan. Lubricants and coolants come from elsewhere in Mexico. Locally the company buys only screws, tools, and janitorial supplies. The company gets some replacement parts locally through local tool and die makers. Although the company has sought locally manufactured foam and plastic boxes, it could not find suitable local suppliers and therefore sources these packaging materials from the United States.

Plants Associated with a Local *Grupo* in Monterrey

The strategies of Monterrey's industrialists in coping with the fall of the internal market since 1982 have also varied. Some are adapting by becoming suppliers to U.S.-owned automobile plants in Saltillo.[7] The ones in our survey had all adopted a strategy of setting up a maquiladora, mostly as a minority partner with their U.S. clients, sometimes selling out totally to the U.S. clients, occasionally retaining total ownership, and in one case setting up nominal U.S. headquarters on the Texas border. Sourcing, marketing, and technology strategies have also varied.

USEM (Emerson Electric)

USEM is an outgrowth of a local company that had spent twenty-five years as a domestic producer in an industry that is well developed in Monterrey—metal mechanics. In 1986 Motores U.S. de México formed a partnership with Emerson Electric and founded two maquiladoras to remain viable in the new open economy. Emerson provided 99.6 percent of the equity capital in each one. USEM, one of these maquiladora plants, manufactures electric motors and steel machine castings for electric motors, all for export to North America (5 percent to Canada). USEM applied for permission to sell up to 20 percent on the internal market but was denied.

The plant is a manufacturing operation—not assembly. Only 6 percent of the total production costs are for labor. The 488 line workers are all males. The average worker has a primary school education only (6 years) and receives four to eight weeks of training on the job. Fifteen percent of the workers are temporaries.

The plant uses traditional nonautomated production machinery that is all on consignment from Emerson. Management has, however, begun to introduce a system of continuous quality control and worker participation in problem diagnosis (Phil Cosby system), as well as quality circles, even though there is still a separate quality control department. The management has not introduced JIT or worker rotation. Worker productivity is lower than at Emerson's parallel plants in Arkansas and Mississippi, not because of error rates, but because of more antiquated technology.

The amount of domestic content is high for a maquiladora—15 percent. Some of the exports do not qualify for TC 806/807 because of high domestic content, and some actually qualify for GSP because they have more than 35 percent domestic content. Nevertheless, the local content could be much higher. Half the national inputs come from Monterrey, primarily iron castings. The remaining iron castings come from elsewhere in Mexico: Torreón, Aguascalientes, Mexico City, and Saltillo. Laminated steel, copper wire, and steel bearings used to be sourced locally in Monterrey, but now all come from the United States (in part to avoid duties on entry into the United States and in part because exchange rates have made U.S. prices more attractive). Steel bars also come from the United States, despite local availability. Even metal stamping and tool and die work is sourced in the United States despite local availability, according to the general manager, because the exchange rate makes them too expensive locally.

The management is pleased with the infrastructure, availability of skilled labor and engineers, and the lower turnover rate (1 percent per month) in Monterrey compared to the border. The main problem with the Monterrey location, however, is dissatisfaction by the expatriate management with living in Monterrey as opposed to the border, where they can live in the U.S. twin city and commute.

Compañía de Motores Domésticos (Emerson Electric)

The other maquiladora set up in 1986 by Motores U.S. de México in partnership with Emerson is Compañía de Motores Domésticos. Unlike USEM, this one does pure assembly of electric motors, all for export to the United States, with all the goods entering under TC 806/807. It is a labor intensive operation, with 60 percent of its 263 line workers being women. Training for the workers in this plant averages only five days, compared to three months for the sister plant. The workers have the same average level of formal schooling—about six years of primary school. The labor turnover rate is higher in this plant—3 to 4 percent monthly. But in neither plant does the general manager consider that there is a labor problem.[8]

This plant uses all new machinery but none of it is automated. The management has no intention to introduce second generation management methods such as JIT, worker rotation, worker participation in problem diagnosis, or quality circles. The only exception is that within the next two years the management plans to introduce SPC.

All of the productive inputs and services come from Emerson's plant in Independence, Kansas.

Elizondo, Planta 1 (Carrier)

In 1986 the Elizondo group reorganized one of its plants for export using foreign capital. It proposed to Carrier, the air-conditioning manufacturer based in Syracuse, New York, with whom the group had done substantial business, that Carrier buy out the plant. Carrier agreed and became the sole owner of Elizondo, SA de CV, Planta 1, manufacturing evaporator coils and cabinets for Carrier's home air-conditioning units in the United States.

This is a manufacturing operation with all male workers (320 line workers). The operation is moderately capital intensive, with 9 percent of total production costs going to labor. Average training time is one month, and average formal education of the line workers is

9 years (secondary education). A very large 45 percent of the labor force is composed of temporary workers.

There is just a small use of computer-controlled production machinery with no plans to automate any further. However, the plant is in the process of implementing the more qualitative changes of flexible production: just-in-time inventorying (already down to 5 to 7 days of inventory on hand), worker rotation, and worker participation in problem diagnosis, quality control (Crosby method), and quality circles.

The plant is moderately integrated into the local economy. Almost all the 35 percent of inputs that are domestic come from Monterrey. One of its three major inputs, galvanized steel, is manufactured totally in Monterrey. Twenty percent of another of the top three inputs, aluminum fin stock, comes from Monterrey with the rest coming from the United States. Finally, all the copper tubing comes from the United States and Japan, and plastic resins from the United States. Plastic injection molding comes mainly from the United States (New York), a part from Monterrey, and some of it is done in-house. All metal stamping is done in-house. Tool and die services are done partly in-house and partly obtained from providers in Monterrey.

As in other cases, the plant was already here when it became a maquiladora. The production manager said that they are pleased with the location, because of proximity to the United States and easy transportation links—trucking, air, and rail. Gas and water availability are adequate. Proximity to suppliers is better than at the border. Administrative personnel and skilled workers are readily available, and turnover among unskilled workers is low. The worst problem cited by the production manager was worker absenteeism. Nevertheless, he characterized the labor situation in Monterrey as good.[9]

Mextron Electronics

PRODENSA, a Monterrey firm (100 percent local capital), established Mextron Electronics as a shelter operation in Monterrey, but with nominal headquarters in McAllen, Texas. As a shelter type of maquiladora, the plant provides an assembly service for multiple clients who provide the inputs, technology, technical assistance, and often the machinery, and enters all the products into the United States under TC 806/807. Almost all of PRODENSA's contracts for the Mextron plant are now with a single client, Illinois Tool Works, Inc., in Chicago.[10] Mextron assembles computer boards and switches for keyboard keys with 70 line workers, 95 percent of whom are women with 9 years of formal schooling and one month of on-the-job training on average.

This plant is an example of a labor intensive but advanced flexible producer. Seventy percent of total production costs are for labor. Nevertheless, it uses a moderate degree of computer-controlled production machinery, primarily in producing key switches. The plant uses JIT totally, maintaining no inventory of inputs. It uses worker rotation or multiskilling to a high degree and uses workers extensively in quality control, problem diagnosis, and even machinery maintenance. The plant does not use temporary workers. The management has already implemented a moderate degree of continuous quality control and SPC and is in the process of expanding both.

Local linkages from this firm are scarce. The capacitors, resistors, and chips come from Taiwan, Singapore, and the United States; the circuit boards from the United States; and keys and switches from the United States (El Paso) and Taiwan. While PRODENSA tried to use domestic plastic injection molding for the keys, the general manager said that while the quality and quantity were adequate, the servicing and follow-up were not. There are no local productive services used; not even packaging material is bought locally. The only possible link is that PRODENSA is considering subcontracting some of the Mextron production to another firm in its *grupo*.

PRODENSA likes the Monterrey location because of the availability of skilled workers, low turnover rates, and good union situation (its workers belong to FSI). The general manager also highlighted the existing industrial base and infrastructure as an attraction, yet this attraction has not turned into greater interaction with the local industrial base than would be typical along the border. The main problems with the Monterrey location are truck transportation costs to the border.

Mextron does not sell any of its output in Mexico, not because there is no market, but because it does not wish to negotiate the red tape required to get permission for a maquiladora to sell on the internal market.

Completely Foreign-owned Plants in Monterrey

Rogers Electronics

Rogers Corporation of Connecticut with division headquarters in Tempe, Arizona, originally had a maquiladora in Agua Prieta, Sonora—an electronics assembly plant with no Mexican inputs. High labor turnover rates and a shortage of skilled and professional workers were two reasons that prompted the parent company to move the plant to Monterrey in 1988. The management has been pleased with the peaceful labor situation in Monterrey.[11]

However, another important reason for moving to Monterrey was to have access to an international airport that makes exporting to Europe easier than in many places along the border. The Rogers maquiladora sends only 60 percent of its output to the United States. The rest goes primarily to Europe and also to Asia (Singapore and Australia). The Monterrey location will also be more convenient for supplying the growing Mexican electronics market, which is centered in Guadalajara. The firm has been granted permission to sell up to 20 percent of its output in Mexico and has contracts to begin supplying IBM and Hewlett Packard (export-oriented but non-maquiladora U.S.-owned electronics plants) in Guadalajara.

The main drawbacks to a Monterrey location are public transportation and telephones. The company has solved the latter by installing private telephone and computer lines to Tempe.

The Rogers maquiladora is primarily an assembly operation, with 450 line workers—95 percent women—putting together capacitors for computers. All the products that enter the United States do so under TC 806/807. Forty percent of total production costs are for labor. Workers receive about one month of training. Most of them have had some secondary school education, averaging 9 years of formal schooling. This educational background is necessary, according to the manager, because the workers work with numbers and drawings.

The company uses only one computer-controlled production process—the ovens—and does not plan on introducing any further automation. Moreover, it has no intention of introducing any flexible production methods on the administrative level other than multi-skilling of the line workers. Rogers has a parallel plant in Tempe where the productivity is higher, not because of greater automation, but because the Monterrey plant—less than one year old at the time of the interview—is still on the learning curve, according to the manager.

Despite the move to a major manufacturing center, the Rogers maquiladora sources no productive inputs locally. The components for the capacitors come from company plants in Arizona (where the copper tape is cut and chips are manufactured) and Tennessee, while some specialized packaging material comes from Texas (Dallas).

Other packaging material—plastic bags and boxes—are sourced in Monterrey, and the company does use local tool and die services.

Calmar (Plastics)

Calmar is another of the U.S.-owned maquiladoras not associated with a local *grupo*. Typical of this group, it uses no domestic content at all. What is unusual is its emphasis on advanced flexible production methods, including the use of computer-controlled equipment, despite being a labor-intensive assembly operation. Assembling plastic parts and springs to make spray dispensers for plastic bottles, 65 percent of total production costs are for labor. Nevertheless, the factory uses computer-controlled machines to sand and polish the plastic pieces to very exact specifications. The engineering staff has made innovative adaptations of these machines to fit its needs. The management rotates each worker through multiple tasks (multiskilling), has introduced worker participation in problem diagnosis, continuous quality control, and machine maintenance, and is planning on developing worker participation further. The plant also has established the use of SPC and continues to upgrade it. The general manager said they actually advise the home office in management procedures. The only major feature of flexible production the management has not been able to introduce as yet is JIT. The factory still maintains a two week supply of stocks in order to respond to orders as they come in.

The factory boasts a higher worker productivity than the home plants, even though it uses 40 percent temporary workers. The 200 line workers, 95 percent of which are women, receive between a week and a month of on-the-job training. They have on average nine years of formal education (i.e., some secondary schooling).

With dual headquarters in Los Angeles and Kansas City, Calmar chose the Monterrey location in 1986 because of its proximity to Midwest clients, including the Kansas City home plant, which provides the majority of inputs (all the springs and some of the molded plastic parts). The firm was also attracted by the skill level of the line workers, the availability of local engineers, and the cultural orientation of Monterrey toward the United States. The general manager's main complaints are the scarcity of skilled workers and the distance to the Los Angeles home plant, which provides parts of the molded plastic inputs.

Mattel/Montoi

Mattel, whose headquarters are in Hawthorne, California, already had one maquiladora in Tijuana when it opened the Monterrey plant in 1985. There it assembles and packages plastic toys with a traditional labor intensive operation using 80 to 90 percent temporary workers during the primary production season of July, August, and September (in preparation for Christmas). Ninety percent of the 200 line workers are women with an average of only one week of training on the job and nine years of schooling. All of the output goes back to the United States.

The attraction of Monterrey was the local work ethic,[12] local suppliers (packaging material and plastic molding), good technical personnel, and lower labor costs than at the border (the director of human resources said it was 13 percent cheaper in Monterrey than at the border). On the other hand, distance to the border is a problem (a transportation expense) and the management has had a history of bad relations with the CTM, to which their workers belong.

The main input, plastic resin, comes solely from the United States. However, much of the second most important input, packaging material, is sourced domestically.[13] The Monterrey plant does final packaging of the finished toys. Nearly half the packaging material (primarily carton) comes from Mexico, with half of that from Monterrey, the remainder from Mexico City and Querétaro. The foreign packaging material comes from the United States, primarily Dallas, which is also the source of some plastic pieces. Decals and photos for applying to the toys come from both the United States and Japan. Plastic molding is done both in the plant and by local Monterrey providers. Tool and die work is done in-house. No metal stamping is required.

In terms of second generation or flexible characteristics, the plant uses no computer-controlled production machinery or JIT. However, it has introduced a quality improvement process that is similar to quality circles. Even though the workers work on traditional production lines, they do rotate through various functions as each worker follows several toys from the beginning to the end of the production line. The plant also employs continuous quality control.

Mattel has parallel plants in Europe, Asia, and South America. The director of human resources reports that worker productivity at the Monterrey plant (in terms of output per person hour) compares very favorably.

Border Plants

All the border plant managers surveyed except one (Sanyo) indicated they were happy with their border location despite great dis-

satisfaction with high labor turnover rates. None of the border maquiladora managers surveyed except one (Sanyo) said his company
would even consider an interior location.[14] The main reason cited
was that an interior location would mean increased distance, time,
and cost to the United States, which is their primary—if not sole—
market and source of inputs, as well as the location of their headquarters. Also many border managers perceive infrastructure, services, and labor force in the interior to be inadequate. While almost
every border plant surveyed uses no productive inputs or services
from Mexico or the twin city, sells no products in Mexico, and has
created no local spin-offs, there is variation in the decision as to
what extent to adopt second generation flexible production methods. The following cases exemplify these differences.

Juárez

Delmex (Delco, General Motors)

One of the older U.S.-owned automotive maquiladoras (established
in 1973), this General Motors plant has 1,350 line workers (75 percent female, 1,200 unskilled) that assemble electronic parts for automobiles. No longer a typical labor intensive, low technology operation, the plant has adopted a number of second generation
characteristics: a moderate use of computer-controlled production
machinery, a high degree of JIT, with both input stocks and in-
process stocks, some worker rotation or multiskilling, and some
use of SPC and continuous quality control, but no worker participation in problem diagnosis, maintenance and repair of machines,
or quality control. The management considers the plant to be slightly
more capital intensive than labor intensive and to do more manufacturing than pure assembly.

No productive inputs or services are sourced in Mexico or at the
border in either Juárez or El Paso. All the inputs come from the
Delco plant in Chicago; all the outputs go back to the United States
as well.

Conductores y Componentes Eléctricos (Packard)

This U.S.-owned maquiladora started in 1978 assembling electric
harnesses for cars. Only 40 percent of the 1,500 workers are female.
The technology is rather traditional: no computer-controlled production machines, no JIT, no multiskilling, no worker participation

in quality control or diagnosis of problems. Labor accounts for 60 percent of total production costs. Nevertheless, the plant has adopted continuous quality control and SPC to a high degree.

All productive inputs and services come from the parent company in Warren, Ohio, except for a few tools and oils that are bought (but not made) in El Paso.

Nuevo Laredo

Barry de México (Dearfoam Slippers)

Another of the older U.S.-owned maquiladoras (established in 1971), the Barry plant with its 1,300 workers, 80 percent of which are female, continues to employ traditional technology with respect to machinery. It uses no JIT, very little worker rotation, and very little worker participation in problem diagnosis, maintenance and repair of machines, or quality control. Nevertheless, management has introduced a high degree of continuous quality control and SPC. The twin plant in Laredo does the cutting of the cloth, which then gets shipped to the Nuevo Laredo plant for stitching.

No productive inputs or services are sourced in Mexico or the twin cities.

Tricon de México

This U.S.-owned auto seat plant opened in 1986. It employs 250 line workers, 93 percent of which are women. The plant uses traditional production technology and no JIT. The plant does use multiskilling and worker rotation to a high degree; worker participation in quality control and machine maintenance to a moderate degree; and worker participation in problem diagnosis to some degree. The plant also uses continuous quality control and SPC to a high degree.

All the productive inputs and services are sourced in the United States. Only some industrial oils and cleaning articles manufactured in Monterrey are purchased locally.

A. C. Nielsen de México

This is one of the oldest service maquiladoras, established in 1968 to sort and count manufacturers' coupons that consumers turn in with their retail purchases. The 940 workers are 95 percent female, and 80 percent are temporary. The counting takes place on computers, but each worker is responsible for only one task and does not participate in problem diagnosis, machine maintenance and repair, or quality control. Nevertheless, the management of this U.S.-owned plant has implemented a high degree of continuous quality control and SPC.

No inputs are purchased locally or elsewhere in Mexico.

Tijuana

Mutsutech

Begun in 1988, this Japanese plant with home office in Osaka has 51 percent Mexican capital. It manufactures plastic parts for televisions using plastic injection molding. Almost all the forty-five line workers are men and are not unionized. The plant supplies other Japanese maquiladoras in Tijuana (Sanyo, Matsuchita, and Hitachi). The technology is second generation, with a high degree of continuous quality control and significant ("moderate") use of both computer-controlled production machinery and worker participation in quality circles and quality control. SPC was just being implemented, however, at the time of the interview in 1989. The operation is basically manufacturing as opposed to assembly and rather intensive in capital. The productivity per worker is still lower than in the parallel plant in Japan.

The main input, plastic resin, comes from Los Angeles and Osaka. There are no local or Mexican inputs or productive services used.

Video-Tec (Sony)

This Japanese plant, also begun in 1988, is one of several Sony maquiladoras in Tijuana making televisions, VCRs, and compact disc players. The 370 line workers, 80 percent of which are women, assemble video cassettes and audio cassettes for shipment to distributors in the United States. The supervising manager characterized the plant as using a high degree of computer-controlled production machinery (probably to make the plastic cassette holders from plastic resin), a high degree of JIT (with one week of inventory on hand), and a high degree of both continuous quality control and SPC. The plant also uses worker participation in quality control and quality circles to a moderate degree and is in the process of extending worker participation to machine maintenance. The manager characterized the plant as being primarily a manufacturing rather than strict assembly operation and more intensive in capital than labor. Labor productivity compared to the twin plant in Brazil is about the same. The manager did not offer a comparison of his plant's worker productivity to the Sony plant in Piedras Negras (this plant, which also assembles video and audio cassettes, has brought in highly roboticized machines for making plastic cassette holders, rather than importing the holders from Japan as it did previously).

The main inputs all come from the United States or abroad: magnetic tape, resin, and plastic holders. Even metal stamping comes from Japan. No productive inputs or services from Mexico or the twin city are used.

The main reason for locating in Tijuana as opposed to elsewhere in Mexico is proximity to U.S. distributors and maritime ports in San Diego and Los Angeles. Worker turnover is the main problem with the location, but otherwise the labor situation is favorable and the company would choose again to locate in Tijuana. The plant's workers are not unionized.

Sanmex (Sanyo)

The Sanyo manager was the only respondent who was dissatisfied with the border location. On the other hand, the Sanyo plant, established in 1982, is the only one that sells a good part of its output on the Mexican market; that is, it is the only example of a partial maquiladora in our border sample. This Japanese plant manufactures and assembles vacuum cleaners. Only half its production is under maquiladora legal status. The rest is sold in Mexico (40 percent) and exported to other countries (10 percent) such as Canada, Panama, Hong Kong, and Malaysia. Of the 50 percent produced under maquiladora status, 55 percent goes to the United States and 45 percent to Japan and other countries. This plant has a twin plant on the U.S. side of the border, a distribution warehouse at Otay, California.

This older Japanese plant has no computer-controlled production machinery, a low level of JIT (although management is trying to improve it), a low level of worker participation in problem diagnosis and quality control, and no SPC (although management plans to introduce it within two years).

Two of the major inputs, plastic resin and fan motors, do come in great part from Mexico, from the Mexico City area. The vacuum motors all come from Japan. Plastic molding is produced in-house. Metal stamping comes partially from Japan and the United States, while part is done in-house.

The Sanyo manager, like the Sony manager, says that proximity to the United States and access to good maritime transportation were the main reasons for locating here. The 295 workers, a third of which are women, are not unionized, and there has been no problem with strikes. However, the Sanyo manager cites lack of infrastructure as a major drawback followed by labor turnover and says the company would not likely relocate in Tijuana if faced with the decision again. Nevertheless, it would take special financial incentives to get it to invest in the interior due to the added communication and transportation difficulties to the United States.

Maxell (Hitachi)

This Japanese company opened its plant in 1987 assembling audio and video cassettes and computer diskettes that enter the U.S. market under TC 806/807. The 260 line workers are 65 percent women and nonunionized. This is the only plant in the border sample to have a twin plant on the U.S. side of the border that plays a production role: The plant at Otay prepares part of the material that is assembled in the Tijuana maquiladora.[15]

This plant uses a low degree of computer-controlled production machinery; a fairly high degree of JIT, which management is trying to improve further; some multiskilling of workers; and a moderate degree of worker participation in problem diagnosis and quality control. The plant utilizes a high degree of both continuous quality control and SPC.

The Maxell plant is an assembly operation, rather than manufacturing, bringing in plastic cassette holders already made from the U.S. headquarters in Atlanta and the magnetic tape already cut at the twin plant in Otay. No other productive inputs are sourced locally or elsewhere in Mexico. Some plastic molding comes from Otay and metal stamping from elsewhere in the United States.

While the Maxell manager characterizes the labor turnover in Tijuana as "horrible" and public infrastructure, especially telephone and local transportation, as "inadequate," he would still choose to locate in Tijuana again. Nevertheless, he pointed out, other plants are closing and returning their production lines to their home countries.

7. Export-led Development and Local Linkages: The Policy Implications

While it is true that foreign assembly industry tends to be an enclave, this analysis of maquiladora transaction patterns shows that the lack of linkages is not due to some inherent structural characteristic that transcends policy intervention. While it is true that the new wave of flexible production in maquiladoras generates fewer linkages than ever, the analysis shows that the flexible producers in Guadalajara still generate some important linkages that can be encouraged and replicated. While it is true that national Mexican policy, especially in computers and technology transfer, has helped create some local linkages, this analysis makes it apparent that most of the obstacles and opportunities are rather specific to both place and sector. These obstacles and opportunities should be identified and treated at the local level with finely tuned efforts aimed at transforming each sectoral cluster of firms into an effective transactional network.

The transactional analysis of chapter 5 identifies a set of existing linkages that could be replicated or strengthened. For example, if one electronics maquiladora is using local tool and die services, it is possible that another one with the right information and contacts would do so also, or if one apparel plant is able to sell abroad with local thread, dyes, and glues, then quite likely others could. Their U.S. clients may not be aware of the availability of these inputs, or perhaps the producers need bridge loans to enable their acquisition until revenues start coming in.

The transactional analysis also identifies a set of missing linkages that could be established. If one electronics firm is manufacturing a component needed by another that currently sources the item abroad, a new local linkage could be created, or if there is sufficient local demand for a specialized input that is currently imported, an opportunity for a new provider to fill the need locally could be pointed out. Alternatively, a potential local supplier of a maquiladora could become a subcontractor with an actual foreign supplier, agreeing to provide a certain quantity and quality of goods to the maquiladora by a certain date at a price that would allow the foreign supplier a profit and insulate the maquiladora from the risk of trying a new local supplier.

When private sector initiative for creating these linkages is lacking, then local public sector support is crucial. The following sections describe some cases of effective networking with both craft producers and electronics manufacturers, showing the interplay between public and private sector.

Building Networks among Crafts Producers

The Emilia Romagna region in north-central Italy successfully developed from a branch plant economy in the 1970s to one of independent small producers in the 1980s (Friedman 1987; Hatch 1987). The transformation began as the large firms restructured, laid off their strongly unionized employees, and began to subcontract much of their work. Some of the unemployed workers began to establish small craft shops that were at first little more than sweatshops of cheap labor subcontracting on terms set by the large firms. "In time, however, more and more small shops escaped from these limitations by developing an alternative set of ties: they learned to balance vertical connections to the big factories with horizontal linkages to other small companies like themselves" (Hatch 1987: 5). Supported by their own networks, the small firms learned to use their comparative advantage of flexibility. They combined the production lines of different small producers to produce finished or nearly finished products and larger outputs. They took advantage of market niches in which a small scale was not a technological disadvantage.

The craft manufacturers gradually increased the technological level of the machines used. "I began with a simple sewing machine, the kind you see at home," explained one woman owner of a small specialty sewing company for knitwear industry in Capri interviewed by Hatch. "Then step by step I got real sewing machines and now I have electronic ones." The firms began to do more of their own work rather than subcontracting and began to export their own products as they found market niches abroad. In the case of textiles they were able to diversify their client base away from Germany. The economy of north-central Italy now consists of growing industrial districts of small producers in textiles and apparel, shoes, machine tools, agricultural equipment, and a few others. Wages have risen to 175 percent of the national average and half the craft workers are now unionized (Hatch 1987).

One of the central ingredients to the region's success was the development of transactional clusters into effective organizations or networks aimed at helping member firms. The local public sector (municipal and regional government) has played a catalyst role in helping to establish networks, although the initiative and development have largely been private, by the companies themselves.

In Emilia Romagna, Hatch has identified four trade associations that serve craft manufacturers.[1] They provide a wide range of business services such as payroll, billing, inventory control, general accounting, and legal services. They offer management training and group insurance, gather and disseminate market information, represent member firms in trade shows in Italy and abroad, help create consortia or joint ventures among member firms so that they can respond to large contract opportunities, and negotiate industrywide union contracts for the small producers on a national and regional basis.

Some of the trade associations help member firms gain access to financing—not subsidized government loans, but market rate private sector loans. An individual small craft manufacturer typically has difficult access to traditional bank financing at any interest rate because of the high risk and high transaction cost associated with lending to a small firm. The National Confederation of Artisans (CNA) has established loan guarantee consortia in Emilia Romagna. A consortium reduces the risk to the lending institution by guaranteeing the loan and thus also reduces the transaction cost because the bank does not have to investigate the particular borrower's credit worthiness. The loan guarantee consortium, meanwhile, can evaluate at a very low cost the credit worthiness of the loan applicant because the CNA has probably been keeping her books for years and she is known in the local chapter (Brusco and Righi 1987).

The trade associations have also provided special management assistance for new firm start-ups. For example, ECIPAR, the training arm of the CNA, teaches administrative skills to fledgling entrepreneurs, assists them in preparing business plans, handles legal procedures required to open an enterprise, helps to organize financing, and uses network contacts to help set up initial contracts (Hatch 1987).

Gaining access to affordable space with a design that facilitates frequent face-to-face interaction is another area in which the trade unions in cooperation with local government have assisted member firms. In Bologna, the largest city of Emilia Romagna, the municipal government has contracted with the CNA to form consortia of firms in need of space. The municipality builds the infrastructure, then gives a long-term lease to the consortium to develop the land according to its members' needs. In some cases publicly assisted housing has been built nearby to minimize commuting and facilitate the entry of women into the labor force. In the small city of Modena, the CNA has organized groups of users to buy completed developments of "artisan villages" planned and built by the municipality. By 1987, 500 small businesses employing 7,000 workers had been accommodated in these urban villages (Hatch 1987: 8).

Beyond the general assistance of the CNA and other broad trade associations for small manufacturers, there are six sector specific organizations in Emilia Romagna that have been created since 1980 through the cooperation of local government, trade associations, and labor unions. Called Sectoral Service Centers, they are organized as membership corporations to promote marketing and technology transfer geared to the special needs of the particular craft sector. Small as well as large firms in the sector may join. CITER, the textile industry's center, was founded in 1980 with primarily public funding. By 1987, however, it was almost totally supported by its 500 member companies. With a permanent staff of ten, CITER provides current information on world markets, suppliers, and technological change in fibers and production machinery. CITER is helping to develop an affordable CAD system for knitwear design. It sponsors technology demonstrations and group meetings to stimulate peer pressure to modernize (Hatch 1987).

The Italian case is not the only example of craft industry restructuring as a flexible network able to compete in the export market. In Denmark the domestic textile and apparel industry of mainly small producers was declining sharply in the 1970s. During the 1980s it restructured by putting a new emphasis on designing for specialized market niches, maintaining reliable delivery schedules, offering good service, and enhancing quality through worker-management collaboration. By 1987, the Danish textile industry was exporting more than 80 percent of its production (Lundholt 1987: 13).

Networking among firms was a key to their successful restructuring. The director of the Federation of Danish Textile Industries points out that the trade association no longer deals only with the traditional issues of collective bargaining, political lobbying, and "export assistance at the so-called embassy level." She says that "today we offer both small and large member firms comprehensive service in labor law, social law, commercial law, export and sales, technology, international and external environment, education, political lobbying activity, and special services (on a fee-for-service basis) in the fields of credit rating information, collection of bills (both national and international), translation, telex, and the like" (Lundholt 1987: 15).

The Federation of Danish Textile Industries has also emphasized worker training and technology upgrading. To overcome the image of being a low skill industry, the association has introduced vocational training at all levels and started recruiting campaigns in the schools. The association also has a technology institute that helps develop and disseminate suitable new technologies to the members. "Our member companies are now using our services extensively. Usually we are in contact with about half of our 310 members every day" (Lundholt 1987: 15).

Building Networks in the Electronics Industry

There are similar experiences in the case of electronics; for example, in the region of Montpellier in Mediterranean France (Hansen 1989). In the late 1960s IBM established a major manufacturing plant in Montpellier that spawned a cluster of related small and medium-sized enterprises in data processing, robotics, and artificial intelligence. Drawing on this existing cluster, along with some others in which Montpellier already had a competitive advantage, a local network composed of "managers and directors from local universities, research laboratories, corporations, banks, local government, and regional advisory organizations created a regional program designed to facilitate the introduction of new technologies into existing companies, to assist newly arriving companies, and to promote the creation of small and medium-sized enterprises" (Hansen 1989: 14).

In discussing the emergence of Ile-de-France South, another emerging "technopole," Allen Scott (1988) describes how public planning and policy intervention was necessary to bring the ingredients of the growth complex into full functional interrelationship. The Scientific City Association, founded in 1983 with the support of the French government, local planning agencies, and several corporations, provided a collective identity to the area and facilitated contacts and information exchange among the local planning agencies, educational institutions, research laboratories, and private firms. It is planning to offer venture capital services for local entrepreneurs in order to circumvent the conservative attitudes of the established local banking system (Scott 1988: 75). Also, the French government began a program in 1982 to establish regional centers for technology innovation and exchange known as CRITTs. Four CRITTs serve the needs of particular sectoral clusters in the Ile-de-France. They encourage the development of small innovative firms by bringing together researchers and entrepreneurs. The CRITTs help to break the barriers between large scale national technology agendas and the specific "relational practices involving incremental problem-solving in a context of continual mutual readjustment between firms" (Scott 1988: 77).

Building Transaction Networks in Mexico

Drawing on these and similar success stories of building effective local business networks, a strategy emerges that could be tailored to the case of Guadalajara and perhaps elsewhere in Mexico: Mobilize local businesses cluster by cluster, whether in traditional crafts, electronics, heavy manufacturing, or services, to network among themselves and directly with the exterior. The public sector can play a catalyst role at the local or regional level, although implementation should be pursued by the firms themselves. The basic steps are as follows:

1. Analyze transaction networks, looking at who produces what, how, and for whom, what inputs and services are used and who supplies them.

2. Identify gaps in supplier chains—i.e., inputs and services for which there is sufficient local demand but no local production.

3. Create communication networks among the firms. Trade associations are a vital communication link.

4. Encourage trade and industry associations to provide member firms with management assistance, new firm start-up assistance, group procurement, worker training, financial assistance, such as loan guarantees, sector-specific marketing and technology assistance, and physical facilities that promote interaction.

Of course, public policy and planning intervention will probably not be enough to turn clusters of related business into effective transactional networks in some places (e.g., the border) and in others may not be necessary to achieve the same result. Yet Guadalajara, with its longstanding crafts sector "embedded" (Hansen 1989: 17) in the local economy and its endogeneous as well as foreign electronics sector, seems a propitious candidate for effective public sector efforts to create local transactional networks around the maquiladora industry.

Some additional considerations specific to Guadalajara are necessary. The craft sector is the main contributor to the high percentage of local inputs in Guadalajara's maquiladora industry. Yet there is probably a ceiling to local integration of maquiladora craft production that is far below the degree of local integration of domestic craft producers because of the use of client-supplied inputs by the maquiladoras. As a conduit for technology transfer and a solution to capital shortages maquiladora status provides an easy short-term solution. To increase local linkages, however, it would be necessary to develop more independent conduits to the export market that would not require such extensive use of imported inputs. The networking strategy suggested above could be used to create new conduits.[2]

The foreign electronics firms in Guadalajara have established a small local transactions network through generating spin-offs, bringing in captive suppliers, encouraging joint ventures, and using some local productive services. But the network has not extended to endogenous electronics manufacturers, except for one. Public sector efforts to encourage networking in the electronics sector should focus on integrating the endogenous electronics firms among themselves, with the maquiladoras and other foreign electronics firms, and directly to the exterior.[3]

Conclusions

If the Mexican government is to turn the maquiladora industry into a catalyst for domestic development, it must develop geographically and sectorally specific policies for increasing the maquiladoras' local linkages. Local linkages can be created by turning clusters of isolated firms in the same sector into collaborative interacting networks. Clusters of maquiladoras with a high proportion of locally owned firms, especially those who do manufacturing as opposed to pure assembly, show the greatest ability to generate local linkages. The maquiladoras least likely to create local linkages are the growing number of foreign-owned plants using second generation flexible technology, regardless of location. Thus, the most effective starting point for an export-oriented local linkage strategy is not the needs of the foreign maquiladoras, particularly the high tech ones, but rather the needs of the local producers, especially manufacturers, who want to export.

A policy of encouraging foreign maquiladoras to move to the interior will not, by itself, increase the use of domestic inputs noticeably. The foreign-owned maquiladoras of the interior have not on their own created large local supplier networks. Only with finely tuned efforts tailored to particular sectors and locations can Mexico hope to slowly build the transaction networks that can integrate the foreign maquiladoras into the domestic economy.

In the meantime, the maquiladora industry is likely to grow, although paradoxically it may become less and less visible. As trade barriers come down and Mexico integrates itself further into the U.S. economy, which is the likely scenario, the distinction between maquiladora and nonmaquiladora will blur. Growing deregulation of foreign-owned nonmaquiladora exporters and greater accessibility of domestic producers to maquiladora advantages may render the legal distinction meaningless. The fear, however, is that integration of the Mexican economy into the U.S. economy would create the "maquilization" of the entire economy, based on the comparative advantage of low cost labor. Thus it is imperative that the maquiladora industry be transformed into a catalyst for integrated local development. Only in this way could maquiladoras become a transitory measure in an export-led strategy leading to a comparative advantage beyond that of cheap labor.

Appendix 1

Annual Maquiladora Growth Rates by Region, 1981–1989

Year	Border	Region Interior	Jalisco
Plants			
1981–1982	−3.6	−1.4	18.2
1982–1983	3.7	−5.6	0.0
1983–1984	11.6	14.9	0.0
1984–1985	12.9	14.3	7.7
1985–1986	14.5	36.4	14.3
1986–1987	20.3	65.8	56.3
1987–1988	23.1	28.6	n.a.
1988–1989	16.4	28.1	n.a.
Average			
1982–1989	12.4	22.6	16.1

Year	Border	Region Interior	Jalisco
Employment			
1981–1982	−2.8	−4.8	−4.7
1982–1983	19.2	15.4	16.5
1983–1984	31.1	42.8	25.0
1984–1985	5.1	14.0	−17.3
1985–1986	14.1	44.6	2.1
1986–1987	18.4	43.4	13.7
1987–1988	18.9	31.2	n.a.
1988–1989	13.7	27.2	n.a.
Average			
1982–1989	14.7	26.7	5.9

Source: INEGI, Tables 13 and 14, various years.

Appendix 2

Characteristics of Guadalajara's Maquiladoras by Percent of Local Inputs

% Local Inputs	% Nat'l Inputs	Type[a]	Parent Company[b]	Sector	Plant Age[c]	No. of Workers[d]	Computer Use[e]	Just-In-Time Inventorying[f]	% Fem[g]
40	70	M	Local	Toys	5	70	F	F	60
30	50	M	Local	Furniture	2	43	F	F	25
30	35	M	Krups (G)	Appliances	1	24	F	F	95
20	20	A	Local	Footwear	1	120	F	F	60
20	20	M	Local	Footwear	2	15	F	F	15
20	20	A	Local	Furniture	2	12	F	F	60
15	15	M	Local	Textiles	1	8	F	F	100
10	10	M	Local	Jewelry	4	28	F	F	86
10	13	F	Borg Warner	Auto Parts	11	25	B	D	60
6	12	F	Unisys	Electronics	21	790	A	B	80
5	50	M	Renza (SP)	Auto Parts	8	47	F	F	33
5	10	M	Borg Warner	Auto Parts	9	125	C	D	75
2	4	F	Motorola	Electronics	20	2,440	B	D	70
2	4	M	Easterline	Electronics	4	100	F	F	15
1	15	A	Honda (Jap.)	Auto Parts	1	40	E	B	2
0	96	M	Efka Plastics	Plastics	4	97	C	F	80
0	95	M	Reliance Elec.	Auto Parts	8	57	F	D	20
0	15	A	Digital Power	Electronics	2	16	F	B	95

0	10	M	(Mexico-D.F.)	Footwear	12	68	D	E	70
0	10	A	Local	Footwear	7	55	D	E	70
0	0	M	Local	Textiles	11	34	F	F	100
0	0	M	Shizuki (Jap.)	Electronics	2	650	F	A	80
0	0	A	Gen. Instrum.	Electronics	15	500	C	E	90
0	0	M	(U.S.)	Chemicals	2	150	C	F	80

Source: Wilson survey, 1988–1989.

[a] F: Flexible producer; measured as those plants that have substantial use of computer-controlled production machinery. They also exhibit a high degree of other flexible production characteristics.

M: Manufacturer; measured as those plants with low or no use of computer-controlled machinery, but a substantial degree of manufacturing.

A: Labor-intensive assembly plant; measured as those plants with low or no use of computer-controlled machinery and little or no manufacturing.

[b] If foreign, name of parent company and abbreviation of national origin of company are given (except in case of one U.S. parent company whose name could not be determined). Locally owned Mexican firms whose parent company is in Guadalajara are indicated by "local." The one Mexican plant whose headquarters are in Mexico City is indicated by "Mexico-D.F."

[c] Plant age given in years since date operations began.

[d] Line workers.

[e] A, B: Substantial use of computer-controlled production machinery.

C–E: Little or no use of computer-controlled production machinery, but with plans to use more in the near future.

F: No use of computer-controlled production machinery and no plans to introduce it in the future.

[f] Use of just-in-time inventorying, following same scale, A–F, as for computer-controlled production machinery.

[g] Percent of line workers that are female.

Appendix 3

Characteristics of Monterrey's Maquiladoras by Percent of Local Inputs

% Local Inputs	% Nat'l Inputs	Type[a]	Parent Company[b]	Local "Grupo"[c]	Sector	Plant Age[d]	No. of Workers[e]	% Fem[f]	Use of Temps[g]	Training Weeks[h]
100	100	M	Sentek	Yes	Glass	2	60	0	High	8
50	90	M	(McAllen)	Yes	Metal	8	50	0	Low	6
50	50	M	Local	Yes	Food	2	100	90	High	12
34	35	M	Carrier	Yes	Metal	3	320	0	Med	4
25	25	M	Am. Electric		Electric eq.	3	400	65	Med	4
18	35	M	Emerson El.	Yes	Metal	3	488	0	Low	6
10	20	M	(McAllen)		Auto parts	3	60	50	High	8
0	0	A	Mattel		Toys	4	200	90	High	1
0	0	F	Calmar Inc.		Plastics	3	200	95	Med	4
0	0	M	Local	Yes	Food	9	100	80	High	12
0	0	F	(McAllen)	Yes	Electronics	2	70	95	Low	4
0	0	M	Lasting		Ceramics	0	65	50	Low	4

0	0	F	James El.		Electronics	1	48	90	Low	4
0	0	A	Emerson El.	Yes	Electric eq.	3	263	60	Low	1
0	0	A	Rogers El.		Electronics	1	450	95	Low	4

Source: Wilson survey, 1988–1989.

[a]F: Flexible producer, measured as those plants that have substantial use of computer-controlled production machinery. They also exhibit a high degree of other flexible production characteristics.

M: Manufacturer; measured as those plants with low or no use of computer-controlled machinery, but a substantial degree of manufacturing.

A: Labor-intensive assembly plant; measured as those plants with low or no use of computer-controlled machinery and little or no manufacturing.

[b]If foreign, name of parent company is given (all U.S. in this case). Locally owned Mexican firms whose parent company is in Monterrey are indicated by "local." Three locally owned firms have set up nominal company headquarters just across the border in McAllen, Texas. They are indicated by "(McAllen)."

[c]"Yes" indicates the plant is associated with a local industrial conglomerate.

[d]Plant age given in years since date operation began.

[e]Line workers.

[f]Percent of line workers that are female.

[g]Use of temporary workers—Low: less than 25 percent of line workers; Med: 25 to 50 percent; High: greater than 50 percent.

[h]Average number of weeks of on-the-job training a line worker receives.

Notes

2. The Global Assembly Industry

1. The literature on export processing often ignores the U.S. commonwealth country of Puerto Rico as an early example because of its uniqueness. As part of the export-oriented industrialization strategy of Operation Bootstrap, promulgated in the 1950s to develop the island's economy, the Mayaguez industrial zone was built and inaugurated in 1962. Virtually the entire island had duty-free access to U.S. markets, however, and Mayaguez offered little additional incentives. Rising wage rates (Puerto Rico is subject to U.S. minimum wage laws) eroded the island's attractiveness for export processing, and now the government of Puerto Rico is attempting to garner a twin plant role of higher value-added activity with respect to the rest of the Caribbean.

2. The Shannon export-processing zone was created by the government of Ireland in the 1950s in response to the decline of the Shannon international airport as a refueling point for intercontinental air travel. To pursue industrial development, the government realized that the restricted size of Ireland's internal market and its basically agrarian economy necessitated an export-oriented strategy. Ireland's new Industrial Development Authority built the infrastructure for the Shannon industrial zone and marketed it to foreign producers interested in a low tax, low labor cost production site with access to the European market. Wage rates have become high enough now that the development authority is seeking high technology manufacturing for reexport (from speech by Tony Shiels, Industrial Development Authority of Ireland, June 1989, in San Juan, Puerto Rico).

3. Robert Reich (1983) points out a third strategy often followed: restructuring through mergers and acquisitions to maintain paper profit levels.

4. Ruth Pearson (1986) argues that women were particularly sought, not because they are universally dexterous and docile workers, but because working-class women are almost universally socialized to be dexterous and docile and therefore better suited than men to the fine work of component assembly and stitching. She also argues that the supply of low wage women workers in the United States was declining, thus motivating the move to Third World countries. See also Nash and Safa (1980), Nash and Fernandez-

Kelly (1983), and Fernandez-Kelly (1983). Sklair (1989: 172) adds that "docile, undemanding, nimble-fingered, nonunion, and unmilitant workers will be offered the jobs on the global assembly lines, while aggressive, demanding, clumsy, union, and militant workers will not," regardless of sex as soon as employers overcome their stereotypes and find out that women do not have a monopoly on the desired qualities.

5. This international strategy was not limited to assembly, but also included higher value-added manufacturing. The U.S. automobile industry became the leader of this global manufacturing strategy with Ford's "world car" concept of the early 1980s. The concept was ultimately abandoned in the mid-1980s.

6. For workers in advanced countries, the new international division of labor signaled the weakening of organized labor and the loss of jobs and real income. It meant the demise of the big capital/big labor alliance in which workers had been dealt an expanding share of an expanding pie. It meant declining productivity as corporations pursued strategies that did not increase productivity but simply reduced costs. On a public policy level, the new international division of labor accompanied supply side economics, fiscal austerity, measures to deal with protectionist backlashes, and a general weakening of the advanced nation-states' ability to control capital flows.

7. Grunwald and Flamm (1985) point to an earlier beginning of offshore electronic component production: transistor assembly in the early 1960s. Faced with competition from cheap Japanese transistors (Japanese wage rates at the time were much lower than U.S. wages), U.S. producers followed the lead of the Fairchild Corporation, which set up a transistor assembly operation for the U.S. market in Hong Kong in 1961 in order to take advantage of wage rates lower than those in Japan.

8. The alternative of automating component assembly was rejected because of the rapid pace of technological change in the field and the short life span of new products (product obsolescence), which made investment in costly single purpose machinery unattractive. *Flexible* automation (i.e., the use of programmable machinery capable of responding rapidly to changes in product design) could have been attractive, but was not well known at the time, particularly among U.S. manufacturers (see chapter 4).

9. Ironically, in response to "voluntary" import quotas set up by the United States in the mid-seventies, Japanese television manufacturers began to set up assembly plants in the United States, bringing in components from Japan and developing countries.

10. The International Multi-Fiber Agreement promulgated by the United States set quotas on textile and apparel imports that stifled the growth of Mexican and Caribbean assembly operations in these sectors during the 1970s.

11. Examples of public enterprises created in pursuit of import substituting industrialization include electricity generation and distribution, iron and steel, housing, transportation, food distribution, and even foreign ex-

change–generating enterprises such as mining and petroleum to ensure a steady supply of dollars with which to import the necessary industrial inputs and technologies.

12. Fairchild, which already had plants in Hong Kong and Korea, located in Singapore primarily to spread its offshore country risk, rather than to seek lower wage rates, according to Chang (1971).

13. The Kuomintang was composed of Chinese nationalist mainlanders, led by Chiang Kai-chek, who had fled to Taiwan after being defeated by the Communist army of Mao Tse-tung in 1949. The refugees from mainland China—like the Cubans in Miami after the Cuban Revolution—included a high proportion of entrepreneurs, professionals, and educated workers.

14. Note the stark contrast between this 1961 military coup in Korea aimed at instituting an export-led strategy with the military coup in Peru at the same time that was aimed at implementing import substitution. While the United States was actively supporting modernization strategies in Latin America based on import substitution at this time (through the Alliance for Progress program), Cumings claims that in both Korea and Taiwan the United States was actively promoting the switch to export-led industrialization (Cumings 1984: 27).

15. Researchers have since shown that workers' earnings in Hong Kong's manufacturing industry did not keep up with labor productivity increases through the sixties and seventies (Glasmeier 1989: 6).

16. Colombia may also be considered an exception. The government converted several commercial free trade zones to export-processing zones in the early 1970s as part of an export-oriented strategy. While Colombia has generated a substantial export-oriented manufacturing sector, little of it is due to the zones. Currie speculates that the zones were used mainly as a way to avoid duties on imported inputs by domestic firms selling to the domestic market (Currie 1984: 16).

17. The Bataan Export Processing Zone in the Philippines is another example of using assembly industry to develop an undeveloped region. This isolated zone was built in 1969, not as part of a national export-oriented strategy, but as a highly targeted regional development strategy in a country rife with regional, ethnic, and class unrest.

18. U.S. Tariff Items 806/807 may have influenced some firms to locate in Mexico, as opposed to farther away, because of the preferential tax treatment—beyond host country incentives—given to U.S.-made components which were more easily accessible from Mexico. Ruiz and Tiano (1987) argue that the presence of a large pool of young, unemployed women, many unsupported and with dependents of their own, has attracted assembly plants to the northern border of Mexico.

19. In 1987 Haiti remained the lowest-wage nation in the Caribbean. The wage rate was less than two-thirds that of the Dominican Republic: 38 cents an hour compared to 61 cents an hour (*Economist Intelligence Unit Country Report: Cuba, Dominican Republic, Haiti and Puerto Rico* 1 [1987]: 17).

20. The only other sizeable location for assembly processing in Latin America in the 1960s and 1970s was Manaus, the one-time fashionable and thriving freeport in a remote section of the Amazon River in Brazil. Established in 1968, the Manaus Export Processing Zone had over 200 manufacturers at the end of 1983, mainly in electronic and electrical appliances (calculators, color televisions, electric typewriters) and mainly from Japan and Europe. The average wage for unskilled workers in Manaus in 1983 was U.S. $.70 to $.80 per hour (Currie 1984: 211).

21. Other important links are technology transfer and skill upgrading (i.e., labor mobility). Backward linkages, however, are probably the most important because they can become the vehicle for more widespread technology transfer and skill upgrading.

22. Moreover, for U.S. corporations—the principal participants in the global assembly industry—the U.S. tariff items 806/807 provide added incentive to use U.S. components, since local components would be taxed upon entry into the United States.

23. These figures include sales from other firms within export-processing zones as domestic content.

24. Malaysia's proportion of domestic inputs (other than capital goods) in its assembly industry stayed very low, between 3 and 6 percent from 1974 to 1978, although the percentage of local capital goods (excluding construction) increased from 16 to 21 percent over the same years. Spinanger suggests that this rise reflects the increasing purchases of local dyeing machines by textile manufacturers, who are largely local (Spinanger 1984: 79).

25. For complex integrated circuits, only 4 percent of entire cost is assembly (Currie 1984: 21).

26. Particularly in textiles and clothing, firms from Hong Kong, Taiwan, and South Korea have been investing heavily in overseas assembly, especially Malaysia, Indonesia, Thailand, China, Sri Lanka, and most recently the Caribbean. Quota restrictions in the United States and rising wages at home have been the primary motivations.

27. Even in the Shannon region of Ireland, Sklair finds most foreign-owned firms buying few local inputs, despite vigorous efforts by the development authorities to foster local sourcing. Nevertheless, Sklair rates the Shannon experience more highly in terms of technology transfer and local skills upgrading, due largely to the local R&D of some of the foreign firms and the resulting growth of local value added (Sklair 1986).

28. By 1983, Taiwan's science park near Taipei had thirty firms, with another twelve under construction (Spinanger 1984: 78).

29. Korea, for example, has generally kept foreign direct investment to under 10 percent of total long-term credit (Fajnzylber 1981: 122).

30. Partly as a buffer or transition zone from this capitalist bulwark (which China is due to incorporate in 1997) and partly to take advantage of the infrastructure, demand, skills, and capital in Hong Kong, the government set up the Shenzhen Special Economic Zone on the Hong Kong border in 1979.

31. The tax incentives offered in President Reagan's Caribbean Basin Initiative starting in 1984 were more liberal than existing U.S. Tariff Items 806/807 (Bennett 1987: 25). Also, the Twin Plant provision allowed U.S. firms doing assembly in Caribbean countries to repatriate their profits tax free if they had a twin plant in Puerto Rico (and if the host country had signed a tax information exchange agreement with the IRS to monitor drug money flows).

32. Korean corporations have created a negative public image for themselves in the Caribbean, however, because of the way they treat workers.

33. According to U.S. Department of Commerce (Caribbean Basin Initiative Office), the Dominican Republic's manufacturing wage fell to 50 cents a day, not counting benefits, in 1989.

34. The rise of the New Directions movement in the United Auto Workers is a direct expression of this resistance.

35. This observation came from Tchen Tchiang, a Taiwanese doctoral student who is doing a comparison of the assembly industry in Taiwan and Mexico for his dissertation at the University of Texas.

3. The Rise of the New Maquiladoras

1. There was some precedent in the border region for this type of activity. The border state of Baja California Norte, where Tijuana is located, had been a free zone since 1939 and firms there could already operate much like a maquiladora. Also, there were examples of U.S. assembly plants that had been set up elsewhere along the border since the 1950s to take advantage of the cheap labor without special tax incentives from Mexico (Sklair 1989: 28, 48). There were, however, existing tax exemptions from the U.S. side: items 806/807 of the U.S. Tariff Code.

2. The term *maquiladora* is derived from the Spanish word for the amount of corn paid by a farmer to the miller to grind the corn. Similarly, the maquiladora industry uses inputs provided by the client and returns the output to the same client. Along the border the terms *maquila* and *maquiladora* are used interchangeably. In Guadalajara, where much of my fieldwork took place, the term *maquila* refers to subcontracting, or "putting out," labor-intensive activities (e.g., sewing garments) to small workshops or households, with no reference to the special legal status of maquiladoras.

3. Maquiladoras may be set up as a branch plant of a foreign (e.g., U.S.) corporation. Few corporations do this, however, because of high Mexican tax rates on branch plant profits. Consequently, most foreign corporations organize a Mexican corporation (Tarbox 1986: 116). Partnerships (as opposed to joint ventures) under Mexican law leave general partners with unlimited liability and therefore are little used as a legal form for maquiladoras.

4. After 1971 firms in Baja California were no longer allowed to operate as maquiladoras simply by taking advantage of the free zone designation. They had to register as maquiladoras.

5. Since 1980 the GSP subcommittee has begun to delete products upon petition of domestic (U.S.) producers who can prove injury to domestic interests (Schwartz 1987: 11).

6. Some authors, such as Sklair (1989) and Carrillo V. (1989), use the devaluation of 1976 as another turning point. The 1976–1982 period was a transitional period buoyed by the oil boom, as the country moved from an import substitution strategy to a neoliberal strategy.

7. PITEX/ALTEX firms are considered by the 1989 Foreign Investment Regulation as profit centers. They are therefore taxed on profits and are required to sell foreign currency to cover both profits and operating costs. Maquiladoras are considered cost centers, subject to foreign currency coverage only on operating costs. They must pay a small service fee (in lieu of taxes) on operating costs only (*Maquilmex Briefs* 1: 2 [July 1989]: 3–4). In the course of my interviews, I talked to a number of plant managers who had intended to register as, or remain as, maquiladoras, but later decided to change to PITEX.

8. The sectoral shift toward automobile subassemblies is actually understated by Table 3 because some of the electronic assembly is for automobiles but gets counted by the Mexican government under electronics.

9. The growth of interior maquiladoras has caused some excitement in U.S. policy circles as well. The U.S. Congressional Commission on International Migration and Cooperative Economic Development pointed out in their final report in 1990 that the growth of interior maquiladoras could potentially reduce migration to the United States. Clark Reynolds pointed out this possible relationship in 1981 (Reynolds, in Erb and Ross 1981: 165).

4. The Challenge of Flexible Manufacturing

1. For an elaboration of the conceptual framework and historical background about Fordism and post-Fordism, see Moulaert, Swyngedouw, and Wilson (1988), from which this analysis is derived.

2. In Latin America, only a caricature of Fordism—which Lipietz calls sub-Fordism (1982: 41)—developed in the postwar years. While Fordism in the developed countries meant the regulation of already established relationships between wage labor and capital, in Latin America it meant the implantation of wage labor relationships (Lipietz 1982: 34) and the development of a national industrial class. Industrialization through import substitution focused on local assembly of final consumer goods that previously had been imported from developed countries. This narrow branch of industry did not spawn the anticipated multiplier effects in capital goods manufacturing or component production. By the 1960s it was clear in most Latin American countries pursuing import substitution that this "infant industry" was actually an industrial enclave, highly dependent on imported machinery and technology and heavily controlled by foreign capital. It could not generate an authentic integrated national economic base. (See the analysis of the Latin American dependency theorists—e.g., Dos Santos 1971; Cardoso 1969; Quijano 1970). The market for consumer durables in

Latin America—the bourgeoisie, the middle class, and the labor aristocracy—remained a small elite percentage of a largely impoverished population. The Fordist social contract of the developed countries did not materialize in the "socially disarticulated" (Alain De Janvry's term, 1981) sub-Fordism of the periphery.

3. Of course there is some debate as to whether these changes constitute a profound transformation of productive relations or simply adaptations of basic Fordist mass production relations (Gertler 1988).

4. Schoenberger (1987) has noted an increasing concentration among U.S. auto parts suppliers as a result of the increased competition for fewer and larger contracts. The auto industry, one of the first in the United States to adopt a number of flexible production practices to a substantial degree, has done so just since the early 1980s.

5. In the case of monopsonistic industries, firms will pass to the suppliers as much of the risk in new product development and as much of the cost of quality control and inventory maintenance as possible.

6. While U.S. firms used to dominate the worldwide production of cars and electric/electronic equipment, international competition—particularly from Japan and the big four Asian producers—altered the picture dramatically, forcing U.S. firms to introduce flexible or post-Fordist practices. By 1985 General Motors had more than 4,000 programmable robots; they have largely replaced welders and painters and are increasingly being used in assembly as well (Sanderson 1987: 133). Besides introducing flexible automation, the big three automakers have introduced JIT, quality circles, SPC, and job rotation (Schoenberger 1987).

7. Source: INEGI 1989.

8. In 1985 Sanderson predicted that "roughly forty percent of the revenues and employment that Mexico currently derives from offshore assembly could be affected by new manufacturing technologies within the next half-decade if automation of U.S. electronics operations proceeds at the predicted rate. Component fabrication—which accounted for over 30 percent of Mexico's export-oriented electronics industry—was expected to be at 80 percent automation within five years, board assembly within seven years, subsystem and system assembly (which accounted for 56 percent of electronics exports) within ten to fifteen years" (Sanderson et al. 1987).

9. Schoenberger (1988) raises the how-far-is-far argument by citing the case of the highly automated Saturn plant in Tennessee.

10. Piore and Sabel (1984) and others describe the Third Italy in much more benign terms as an innovative network of small scale flexible producers making short batches of high quality products.

11. Jaikumar found average production runs among U.S. flexible manufacturers to be six times larger than those in Japanese flexible manufacturers; he also found only one-twentieth the number of new products being introduced annually in the U.S. firms and one-sixth the number of total products being produced (Jaikumar 1986).

12. Over the course of my studies of maquiladoras and border economic development, I have interviewed about thirty industry representatives who cite numerous examples of highly automated maquiladoras.

13. Mario Carrillo Huerta, a demographer at El Colegio de México, administered the thirty border interviews with the assistance of Humberto Lona in Juárez.

14. Interior plants are disproportionately represented for a number of reasons. One of the purposes of the survey, in addition to finding the degree of flexible or post-Fordist characteristics, was to explain the higher degree of national integration found among maquiladoras in the interior. It was also felt that interior plants might have a more difficult time adopting flexible characteristics because of greater logistical problems with JIT. Finally, there was a comparative dearth of information on interior maquiladoras.

15. The total number of maquiladora plants in Monterrey is difficult to pinpoint. The list provided us by the local Association of Maquiladoras had fifty-eight plants listed, but included many that were not yet built and many that had registered in Monterrey (because of the particular bureaucratic ease of registering there) but were located along the border or elsewhere. The association itself had only twenty-five local members at the time of the survey (some of which were not maquiladoras, but simply wanted to stay informed). I used the government figure of thirty-four plants as the base (data for June 1988 from INEGI, Secretaria de Programacion y Presupuesto).

16. In the interior it is not unusual to find part-time and temporary maquiladoras (i.e., plants producing primarily for the domestic market that become maquiladoras in order to export when the domestic market is slack, and plants that produce only a portion of their output under maquiladora status). In the latter case, the survey questions were directed at that portion of the plant's operations carried out under maquiladora status. If the plant was not currently utilizing its maquiladora status, it was dropped from the survey.

17. Initially, individual questions on the extent of CAD (computer-aided design), CAM (computer-aided manufacturing), CNC (computer numerically controlled machines), and FMS (flexible manufacturing system) were asked, as well as an overall assessment of the degree to which computer-controlled production machines were being used. Eventually we collapsed the question to just the over-all assessment since CAD and FMS were uniformly rare.

18. Initially the degree of use of JIT was asked with respect to incoming stocks, in-process stocks, and final stocks. Ultimately only incoming inventory procedures were assessed because of their implications for supplier relationships.

19. In their survey of thirty-five electronics maquiladoras, Palomares and Mertens (1987) characterized a plant as automated if it had at least one programmable machine on the shop floor. This is equivalent to a score of "c" or above in our survey. While the manager was allowed to characterize the degree of automation, he had to be able to cite at least one example of a computer-controlled production machine to be given a "c." We required a score of "a" or "b" to consider a plant to be a flexible producer.

Palomares and Mertens found eleven out of thirty-five plants (31 percent) to be automated; we found 41 percent of the electronics plants to have at least one programmable production machine and 31 percent to have substantial ("a" or "b") programmable machinery.

20. On each of these five attributes—multiskilling, worker participation, continuous quality control, SPC, and JIT—all, or all but one, plant scored a "d" or higher. Half the flexible producers show a high—"a" or "b"—presence of all five attributes at once.

21. The one Mexican plant that appears in the sample of flexible producers is a maquiladora set up by one of Monterrey's large industrial groups to do contract manufacturing for a U.S. firm. The plant manager said the Monterrey group has been upgrading the technology and efficiency in the plant in order to sell the plant to the U.S. firm.

22. According to Echeverri-Carroll (1989), the Japanese own only 2 percent of the maquiladoras (compared to 94.5 percent for the United States), yet more than half of their thirty-nine maquiladora plants have been established since 1986.

23. Carrillo V. (1989) documents the increasing femininization of the labor force in the Mexican auto industry as it increases the use of auto part maquiladoras.

24. Our survey did not yield sufficient observations on occupational structure for the flexible producers; therefore, I cite the results from two sectoral surveys done by others.

25. In January 1989, the minimum wage in Juárez was $.50 per hour plus social security benefits of $.28 for a total of $.78 per hour (National Minimum Wage Commission of Mexico 1989).

26. Twenty percent of these plants also use a high degree of multiskilling and nearly half use worker participation. These findings, however, may be due in part to the more artesenal (i.e., pre-Fordist) nature of small-scale labor intensive shops using simple technologies as in pre-industrial putting-out systems.

27. Growth rate measured in terms of ratio of plants established since 1986 to those established prior to 1986.

28. Carrillo V. (1989) calls it a devaluation (desvalorización) of the labor force.

5. Maquiladoras and Local Linkages

1. Note that the official Mexican government data from INEGI, based on monthly reports from all the registered maquiladoras, show a lower usage of domestic inputs than do the Wilson survey results.

2. Pretesting of the survey instrument along the border showed these three productive services to be the most sought after by the maquiladoras.

3. Among craft-related sectors in the border sample, only three plants were identified, two in footwear and one in apparel. Only one of the three— one of the footwear plants—identified itself as primarily a manufacturer

as opposed to assembly plant. All three are large, ranging from 240 line workers to 1,300. None of the three reported any local inputs.

4. Shizuki bought out the old TRW maquiladora in 1987, closed it, then constructed a new plant in 1988.

5. The Kodak plant had been established in Guadalajara in 1966 to make film for the Latin American Market, including Mexico (source: interview with plant manager, December 1988).

6. Paul Castillo, master's candidate in community and regional planning at the University of Texas, identified most of the endogenous electronics firms and conducted interviews with them as part of his master's thesis on technology transfer in the Guadalajara computer industry (forthcoming).

7. Very few maquiladoras anywhere in the sample subcontract. Only one other maquiladora in Guadalajara—a footwear plant—subcontracts as much as Honda does. It seems that the maquiladoras are at the end of the international subcontracting line.

8. The total number of maquiladora plants in Monterrey is difficult to pinpoint. See note 15, chapter 4. I used the government figure of thirty-four plants as the base (data for June 1988 from INEGI, Secretaría de Programación y Presupuesto).

9. We found two maquiladoras that were created by the same local *grupo* as part of its restructuring process using foreign capital: USEM, with Emerson Electric, created a manufacturing maquiladora and an assembly plant maquiladora in 1986, the former making metal castings for electric motors, the latter assembling electric motors. Both export all their production to the United States, the former using GSP and the latter 806/807. There are no supplier relations between the two plants.

10. With respect to local sales, sales to each other, and partial maquiladoras, Monterrey has fewer than does Guadalajara. Only two are partial maquiladoras, with one—S&P Metals (Máquilas Metálicas)—selling 10 percent of its steel profiles as a nonmaquiladora directly to a local manufacturer of trailers. It sells 50 percent of its output as a maquiladora to another firm in its own *grupo*, which then exports it. The other plant, Oranjugos, sells only 20 percent of its fruit concentrate on average as a maquiladora. At any given moment it may be operating totally as a maquiladora if the internal market is not there; at other times it may not be using its maquiladora status at all.

With respect to national versus local inputs, three firms—all manufacturers with high local inputs—report a sizably higher amount of national inputs than local (i.e., a spread of ten or more points). One gets a major component—steel—from Altos Hornos in Monclova, Coahuila. Another gets 50 percent of its iron castings from Torreón, Aguascalientes, Mexico City, and Saltillo. A third gets wire and insulating tape from elsewhere in Mexico.

11. There were a total of nineteen Japanese maquiladoras in Tijuana in 1989 according to Echeverri-Carroll (1989).

12. We were unable to determine the national origin of this supplier.

13. While not included in this survey, the Sony plant in Piedras Negras was one of the plants I visited during the pretest of the survey instrument.

6. From Motorola to Mextron

1. All information is from the Wilson field survey of 1988/89 and follow-up interviews in late 1991, except where indicated.

2. JIT is applied primarily to in-process work at the Guadalajara plant.

3. The plant made 85 percent of Unisys' cables before it was closed in 1991.

4. While all of the plant's output is sold to the United States, none of the goods enter with TC 806/807 due to the low percent of U.S. content, the high domestic content, and the high value added from the manufacturing process.

5. The plant employed only twenty-four line workers in 1989—all skilled—but this was expected to double by 1991 when a second shift was to be added.

6. Unfinished drills enter the United States under 806/807. The finished drills do not. Tulon had the opportunity to sell to the Mexican market but decided not to.

7. Source: interview with former production manager of the large Ramos Abispe General Motors plant, who cited companies from the *grupo* Alfa as an example of this strategy (March 1989, Monterrey).

8. In both plants the workers belong to a local union, FSI. The manager said that CTM is more problematical than FSI.

9. The workers in this plant belong to the local union, FSI.

10. PRODENSA is in the process of converting Mextron into a subcontracting operation for the Chicago firm.

11. Its workers are unionized. They belong to the CROC.

12. This is curious since most of the plant's labor force is young female labor market entrants.

13. I have considered packaging material throughout this study to be a nonproductive input; however, in the case of plastic toys the packaging can be considered a significant part of the value added.

14. The question was phrased in two ways: "What elements do you consider would have to exist before your company would invest in an interior state of the country?" and "If you could take the decision over, would you choose again to locate in this city?" The answer in all border plants responding to the question (except Sanyo) was that there were no elements that would make it attractive to leave the border. All (except Sanyo) said that they would remain in their present border city if they had to make the decision again.

15. If this plant is like the Sony cassette plant in Piedras Negras, the magnetic tape rolls are cut to the desired width at the U.S. twin plant, then shipped to the maquiladora for assembly into cassette holders. The Piedras Negras manager said that the cutting could be done more cheaply

in the maquiladora and that it was primarily for public relations that they maintained a productive twin plant on the U.S. side (interview, 1988).

7. Export-led Development and Local Linkages

1. Italian law defines craft manufacturers, or artisan firms, as businesses with up to twenty-two workers and a full-time owner/operator (Hatch 1987: 7).

2. Why even bother with small craft firms as a source of employment? Young small firms have a high failure rate. They produce low wage, low quality jobs. Their existence is dependent on demand by large firms who subcontract out to them. Escobar points out that in Guadalajara many of the local large firms are former small craft shops, that the craft producers were until the crisis of 1982 regularizing employment conditions, and that the craft sector has been a long term source of vitality, including a channel of upward mobility for workers from employee to owner. Gabayet adds that they also present a flexible source of income for female workers.

3. Monterrey presents a different set of circumstances. Since much of the large-scale maquiladora industry in Monterrey is not foreign-initiated, its phenomenal growth should be seen largely as a short-term strategy by local economic groups to survive, restructure, and enter the export market. To increase local sourcing in the long run will require, as for the Guadalajara craft producers, a more autonomous conduit to the exterior.

Bibliography

Baird, Peter, and Ed McCaughan. "Hit and Run: U.S. Runaway Shops on the Mexican Border." *North American Congress on Latin America (NACLA) Report*, Berkeley, Calif. July–August 1975.

Balassa, B. "The Changing International Division of Labour in Manufactured Goods." World Bank Staff Working Paper No. 329, 1979, Washington, D.C.

Barrera, Eduardo. "Advanced Telecommunications between Mexico and Texas: The Example of Maquiladora Programs." Austin: Center for Research on Communications, Technology, and Society, University of Texas, November 1988.

Bennett, Karl. "The Caribbean Basin Initiative and Its Implications for CARICOM Exports." *Social and Economic Studies* 36:2 (1987).

Bluestone, Barry, and Bennett Harrison. *The Deindustrialization of America*. New York: Basic Books, 1982.

Boyce, James E., and Manab Thakur. "Participative Management in Mexico II." *Business Mexico* (September 1988): 22–28.

Brusco, Sebastiano. "The Emilian Model: Productive Decentralization and Social Integration." *Cambridge Journal of Economics* 6 (1982): 167–184.

Brusco, Sebastiano, and Ezio Righi, "The Loan Guarantee Consortia." *Entrepreneurial Economy* 6:1 (1987): 11–13.

Brusco, Sebastiano, and Charles Sabel. "Artisan Production and Economic Growth." In ed. Frank Williamson. *The Dynamics of Labor Market Segmentation*, Orlando, Fla.: Academic Press, 1981.

Bustamante, Jorge. "El programa fronterizo de maquiladoras: Observaciones para una evaluación." *Foro Internacional* 16:2 (1975): 183–204.

Cardoso, Fernando H., and Enzo Faletto. *Dependencia y desarrollo en America Latina*. Mexico City: Siglo XXI, 1969.

Carrillo Huerta, Mario, and Victor Urquidi. "Trade Deriving from the International Division of Production: Maquila and Postmaquila Mexico." *Journal of the Flagstaff Institute* 13:1 (April 1989): 14–47.

Carrillo V., Jorge. "Transformaciones en la industria maquiladora de exportación." In *Las maquiladoras: Ajuste estructural y desarrollo regional*, ed. Bernardo González-Arechiga and Rocío Barajas Escamilla.

Tijuana: El Colegio de la Frontera Norte and Friedrich Ebert Foundation, 1989a, pp. 37–54.

———. "Reestructuración en la industria automotriz en México: Políticas de ajuste e implicaciones laborales." Tijuana: El Colegio de la Frontera Norte, January 1989b.

Chang, Y. S. "The Transfer of Technology: Economics of Offshore Assembly, the Case of Semiconductor Industry." United Nations Institute for Training and Research (UNITAR) Research Report, 1971.

Chen, Peter S., ed. *Singapore Development Policies and Trends.* London: Oxford University Press, 1983.

Chu, David K. W. "China's Special Economic Zones: Expectations and Reality." *Asian Affairs* 14:2 (1987).

Cohen, Robert B. "The New Spatial Organization of the European and American Automotive Industries." In *Regional Analysis and the New International Division of Labor,* Frank Moulaert and Patricia W. Salinas. Boston: Kluwer-Nijhoff, 1983, pp. 135–144.

Commission on International Migration and Cooperative Economic Development (Diego Ascensio, Chairman). *Unauthorized Migration: An Economic Development Response.* Washington, D.C.: U.S. Government Printing Office #270-639: QL, 1990.

Cumings, Bruce. "The Origins and Development of the Northeast Asian Political Economy: Industrial Sectors, Product Cycles, and Political Consequences." *International Organization* 38:1 (1984): 1–40.

Currie, Jean. *Export Processing Zones in the 1980s: Customs Free Manufacturing.* Economist Intelligence Unit Special Report No. 190, 1984.

De Janvry, Alain. *The Agrarian Question and Reformism in Latin America.* Baltimore: Johns Hopkins Press, 1981.

Dos Santos, Theotonio. "The Structure of Dependence." In *Readings in U.S. Imperialism,* ed. K. T. Fann and Donald C. Hodges. Boston: Porter Sargent, 1971, pp. 225–236.

Echeverri-Carroll, Elsie. *Maquilas: Economic Impacts and Foreign Investment Opportunities, Japanese Maquilas—A Special Case.* Austin: Bureau of Business Research Monograph No. 1988-1, 1989.

Escobar, Augustín. "The Manufacturing Workshops of Guadalajara and Their Labour Force: Crisis and Reorganization (1982–1985)." Texas Papers on Mexico, No. 88-05, Institute of Latin American Studies, University of Texas at Austin, 1988.

Estall, R. C. "Stock Control in Manufacturing: The Just-in-Time System and Its Locational Implications." *Area* 17 (1985): 129–132.

Fajnzylber, Fernando. "Some Reflections on South-East Asian Export Industrialization." *CEPAL Review* 15 (1981): 111–132.

Fernandez-Kelly, Maria Patricia. *For We Are Sold, I and My People: Women and Industry on Mexico's Northern Frontier.* Albany: State University of New York Press, 1983.

Friedman, Robert E. "Flexible Manufacturing Networks." *Entrepreneurial Economy* 6:1 (1987): 2–4.

Frobel, F., J. Heinrichs, and O. Kreye. *The New International Division of Labor.* Cambridge: Cambridge University Press, 1980.

Gabayet, Luisa. "Regional Development, Industry and Workforce: The Case of Guadalajara and Its Region." Ph.D. dissertation, University of Durham, 1983.

Garrity, Monique. "The Assembly Industries in Haiti: Causes and Effects, 1967–1973." *Review of Black Political Economy* 10 (1974): 203–215.

Gertler, Meric S. "The Limits to Flexibility: Comments on the Post-Fordist Vision of Production and Its Geography." *Trans. Inst. Brit. Geogr.* 13:4 (1988): 419–432.

Glasmeier, Amy. "The Hong Kong Watch Industry." Unpublished paper, University of Texas, Graduate Program in Community and Regional Planning, Austin, Texas, June 1989, 23 pp.

González-Arechiga, Bernardo, and Rocío Barajas Escamilla, eds. *Las maquiladoras: Ajuste estructural y desarrollo regional.* Tijuana: El Colegio de la Frontera Norte and Friedrich Ebert Foundation, 1989.

González-Arechiga, Bernardo, and José Carlos Ramírez. "Los límites del estado mexicano en la promoción de la industria maquiladora." Documentos de Trabajo No. 21, Friedrich Ebert Foundation, Mexico City, 1989.

Griffith, Winston H. "Can CARICOM Countries Replicate the Singapore Experience?" *Journal of Development Studies* 24:1 (1987): 60–82.

Grunwald, J., and K. Flamm, eds. *The Global Factory: Foreign Assembly in International Trade.* Washington, D.C.: Brookings, 1985.

Hansen, Niles. "Dualism, Capital Labor Ratios, and the Regions of the U.S.: A Comment." *Journal of Regional Science* 20:3, (1980): 401–404.

———. "Innovative Regional Milieux, Small Firms, and Regional Development: Evidence from Mediterranean France." Unpublished paper, Department of Economics, University of Texas, 1989.

Hatch, C. Richard. "Learning from Italy's Industrial Renaissance." *Entrepreneurial Economy* 6:1 (1987): 4–10.

Henderson, Jeffrey. "The Political Economy of Technological Transformation in Hong Kong." In Michael Peter Smith, ed., *Pacific Rim Cities in the World Economy* (New Brunswick, N.J.: Transaction, 1989), pp. 102–155.

Hirschman, Albert O. *The Strategy of Economic Development.* New Haven: Yale University Press, 1958.

Ho, Samuel. *The Economic Development of Taiwan, 1860–1970.* New Haven: Yale University Press, 1978.

Holmes, John. "The Organization and Locational Structure of Production Subcontracting." In *Production, Work, Territory: The Geographical Anatomy of Industrial Capitalism,* eds. Allen J. Scott and Michael Storper. Boston: Allen and Unwin, 1986, pp. 80–106.

INEGI. *Estadística de la industria maquiladora de exportación, 1974–1982.* Mexico City: Secretaría de Programación y Presupuesto, 1983.

———. *Estadística de la industria maquiladora de exportación, 1975–1986.* Mexico City: Secretaría de Programación y Presupuesto, 1988.

————. *Estadistíca de la industria maquiladora de exportación, 1978–1988.* Mexico City: Secretaría de Programación y Presupuesto, 1989.

————*Avance de información económica.* Mexico City: Secretaría de Programación y Presupuesto, March 1990.

Inter-American Development Bank. *Annual Report.* 1988.

Jaikumar, R. "Postindustrial Manufacturing." *Harvard Business Review* 64 (1986): 69–76.

Kindleberger, Charles P. *American Business Abroad.* New Haven: Yale University Press, 1968.

Koh, Ai Tee. "Linkages and the International Environment." In *The Singapore Economy Reconsidered,* eds. Lawrence Krause, Koh Ai Tee, and Lee (Tsao) Yuan. Singapore: Institute of South East Asian Studies, 1987.

Krause, Lawrence. "The Government as Entrepreneur." In *The Singapore Economy Reconsidered,* eds. Lawrence Krause, Koh Ai Tee, and Lee (Tsao) Yuan. Singapore: Institute of South East Asian Studies, 1987.

Krause, Lawrence, Koh Ai Tee, and Lee (Tsao) Yuan, eds. *The Singapore Economy Reconsidered.* Singapore: Institute of South East Asian Studies, 1987.

Lee, Dinah. "China: U.S. Importers Aren't Jumping Ship Yet." *Business Week,* May 15, 1989, pp. 45–46.

Lim, Linda Y. C., and Pang Eng Fong, "Vertical Linkages and Multinational Enterprises in Developing Countries." *World Development* 10:7 (1982): 585–595.

Lin, Ching Yuang. *Latin America vs. East Asia.* New York: M. E. Sharpe, 1989.

Lin, Tzong-Biau, and Yin-Ping Ho. *Export Oriented Growth and Industrial Diversification in Hong Kong.* Hong Kong: Chinese University of Hong Kong, 1980.

Lipietz, Alain. "New Tendencies in the International Division of Labor: Regimes of Accumulation and Modes of Regulation." In *Production, Work, Territory: The Geographical Anatomy of Industrial Capitalism,* eds. Allen J. Scott and Michael Storper. Boston: Allen and Unwin, 1986, pp. 16–40.

————. "Towards Global Fordism?" *New Left Review* 132:2 (1982):33–47.

Lo, Shiu-hing. "Decolonization and Political Development in Hong Kong." *Asian Survey* 28:6 (1988): 613–625.

Long, Frank. "Employment Effects of Multinational Enterprises in Export Processing Zones in the Caribbean." Geneva: International Labour Office, Working Paper No. 42, Multinational Enterprises Programme, 1986.

Lundholt, Anne B. "Flexible Networks in the Danish Textile Industry." *Entrepreneurial Economy* 6:1 (1987): 13–15.

Malecki, Edward J. "Technology and Regional Development: A Survey." *International Regional Science Review* 8 (1983): 89–125.

Mertens, Leonard, and Laura Palomares. "El surgimiento de un nuevo tipo de trabajador en la industria de alta tecnología: El caso de electrónico." In *Testimonios de la Crisis I,* ed. Estela Gutiérrez. Mexico City: Siglo XXI, 1988.

Moulaert, Frank and Patricia Wilson Salinas, eds. *Regional Analysis and the New International Division of Labor*. Boston: Kluwer-Nijhoff, 1983.

Moulaert, Frank, Erik Swyngedouw, and Patricia Wilson. "The Geography of Fordist and Post-Fordist Accumulation and Regulation." *Papers of the Regional Science Association* 63 (1988).

Murray, F. "The Decentralisation of Production—The Decline of the Mass-Collective Worker?" *Capital and Class* 19 (1983): 74–99.

Nash, June, and Maria Patricia Fernandez-Kelly, eds. *Women, Men, and the International Division of Labor*. Albany: State University of New York Press, 1983.

Nash, June, and Helen Safa, eds. *Women and Change in Latin America*. New York: Bergin and Garvey, 1985.

Naya, Sheija, Miguel Urrutia, Shelly Mark, and Alfredo Fuentes, eds. *Lessons in Development: A Comparative Study of Asia and Latin America*. San Francisco: International Center for Economic Growth, 1989.

Neff, Robert, and Larami Nakarmi. "Has the Korean Miracle Run Out of Magic?" *Business Week*, July 3, 1989, pp. 38–39.

Palomares, Laura, and Leonard Mertens. "Programmable Automation and New Work Contents: Experiences of the Electronics, Metal Engineering and Secondary Petrochemical Industry in Mexico." Paper presented in the seminar *Automatisation programmable et conditions d'usage du travail*, Paris, April 2–4, 1987.

Pearson, Ruth. "Latin American Women and the New International Division of Labour: A Reassessment." *Bulletin of Latin American Research* 5:2 (1986): 67–79.

Piore, Michael J., and Charles F. Sabel. *The Second Industrial Divide*. New York: Basic Books, 1984.

Quijano, Aníbal. "Dependencia, cambio social y urbanización en Latinoamerica." Cardoso, Fernando, and Weffort, Francisco. In *América Latina: Ensayos de interpretación sociológico-política*, ed. Santiago: Editorial Universitaria SA, 1970, pp. 96–140.

Ramírez, José Carlos, and Bernardo Gonzales-Arechiga. "Los efectos de la competencia internacional en el funcionamiento de la industria maquiladora de exportación en México." *Frontera Norte* 1:2 (1989): 5–34.

Rees, John. "Technological Change and Regional Shifts in American Manufacturing." *Professional Geographer* 31 (1979): 45–54.

Reich, Robert B. "The Next American Frontier." *Atlantic Monthly* (March 1983): 43–58.

Reynolds, Clark. "Notes on U.S.-Mexico Trade Trends: Some Policy Alternatives." In *United States Relations with Mexico*, eds. R. Erb and S. Ross. Washington, D.C.: American Enterprise Institute for Public Policy Research, 1981, pp. 155–178.

Robinson, A. Elizabeth. "A Comparative Study of the Economic Effects of External and Internal Linkages Achieved through Compensatory-Type Investments: The Mexican Automotive Industry." Ph.D. dissertation, George Washington University (International Business), 1988.

Ruiz, Vicki, and Susan Tiano, eds. *Women on the United States–Mexico Border: Responses to Change.* Boston: Allen and Unwin, 1987.

Sanderson, Susan W. "Automated Manufacturing and Offshore Assembly in Mexico." In *The United States and Mexico: Face to Face with New Technology,* ed. Cathryn L. Thorup. New Brunswick: Transaction Books, 1987, pp. 127–148.

Sanderson, Susan W., Gregory Williams, Timothy Ballenger, and Brian J. L. Berry. "Impacts of Computer-Aided Manufacturing and Robotics on Offshore Assembly and Future Manufacturing Locations." *Regional Studies* 21:2 (1987): 131–142.

Sassen, Saskia. *The Mobility of Capital and Labor.* Cambridge: Cambridge University Press, 1988.

Sayer, A. "New Developments in Manufacturing and Their Spatial Implications." Working Paper 49, Urban and Regional Studies, University of Sussex, 1985.

Schive, Chi. "Foreign Investment and Technology Transfer in Taiwan: Past Experience and Future Potential." *Industry of Free China* 70:2 (1988): 1–28.

————. "Linkages: Do Foreign Firms Buy Locally in Taiwan?" Paper presented at the First Convention of East Asian Economic Association in Kyoto, October 29–30, 1988, 24 pp.

Schoenberger, Erica. "From Fordism to Flexible Accumulation: Technology, Competitive Strategies and International Location." *Environment and Planning D: Society and Space* 6:3 (1988): 245–262.

————. "Technological and Organizational Change in Automobile Production: Spatial Implications." *Regional Studies* 21:3 (1987): 199–214.

Schwartz, Scott M. "The Border Industrialization Program of Mexico." *Southwest Journal of Business and Economics* 4:4 (1987): 1–51.

Scott, Allen J. *New Industrial Spaces.* London: Pion Limited, 1988.

Shaiken, Harley, and Stephan Herzenberg. *Automation and Global Production: Automobile Engine Production in Mexico, the U.S., and Canada.* La Jolla: Center for U.S.-Mexican Studies, University of California at San Diego, 1988.

Shaiken, Harley, et al. "The Work Process under More Flexible Production." *Industrial Relations* 25 (1986): 167–183.

Sheard, P. "Auto-production Systems in Japan: Organization and Locational Features." *Australian Geographical Studies* 21 (1983): 49–68.

Sit, Victor F. S. "China's Export-Oriented Open Areas: The Export Processing Zone Concept." *Asian Survey* 28:6 (1988): 661–675.

Sklair, Leslie. *Assembling for Development: The Maquila Industry in Mexico and the United States.* Boston: Unwin Hyman, 1989.

————. "Developmental Effects of Foreign Investment: The Cases of Ireland, China, and Egypt and Their Relevance for Mexico." Center for U.S.-Mexican Studies, University of California at San Diego, working paper, 1986.

Spinanger, Dean, "Objectives and Impact of Economic Activity Zones: Some Evidence from Asia." *Weltwirtschaftliches Archiv* 120: 1 (1984): 64–89.

Stokes, Bruce. "Mexican Momentum." *National Journal*, June 20, 1987, pp. 1572–1578.

Storper, Michael, and Richard Walker. "The Theory of Labor and the Theory of Location." *International Journal of Urban and Regional Research* 7:1 (1983):1–41.

Swyngedouw, Erik A. "Social Innovation, Production Organization and Spatial Development: The Case of Japanese Style Manufacturing." *Révue d'Economie Regionale et Urbaine* 3 (1987): 91–113.

Tarbox, John E. "An Investors' Introduction to Mexico's Maquiladora Program." *Texas International Law Journal* 22:109 (1986): 110–139.

Taylor, Bruce, and R. Yin-Wang Kwok. "From Export Center to World City: Planning for the Transformation of Hong Kong." *Journal of the American Planning Association* 55:3 (1989): 309–322.

Thoumi, Francisco E. "Economic Policy, Free Zones and Export Assembly Manufacturing in the Dominican Republic." In Diego C. Ascencio et al., eds., *Unauthorized Migration: Addressing the Root Causes*. Supplement (Washington, D.C.: U.S. Government Printing Office [0-270-631:QL3], 1990), pp. 245–260.

Vernon, Raymond. *Sovereignty at Bay: The Multinational Spread of U.S. Enterprises*. New York: Basic Books, 1971.

Villarreal Arrambide, Rene. "The New Industrialization Strategy in Mexico for the Eighties." In *Industrial Strategy and Planning in Mexico and the United States*, ed. Sidney Weintraub. Boulder: Westview Press, 1986, pp, 47–59.

Wilson, Patricia A. *NAFTA and the Electronics Industry in Mexico*. Washington, D.C.: U.S. Congress Office of Technology Assessment (Report No. H3-7200.0), 1992, 95 pp.

Womack, James P. "Prospects for the U.S.-Mexican Relationship in the Motor Vehicle Sector." In *The United States and Mexico: Face to Face with New Technology*, ed. Cathryn L. Thorup. New Brunswick: Transaction Books, 1987, pp. 101–126.

Yang, Dori Jones. "China's Economy Is Careening Out of Control." *Business Week*, April 3, 1989, 54–56.

Yang, Dori Jones, and Larami Nakarmi. "Is the Era of Cheap Asian Labor Over?" *Business Week*, May 15, 1989, 45–46.

Index